Stand Out of Our Light

Former Google strategist, now Oxford-trained philosopher James Williams argues that a next-generation threat to human freedom has emerged in the systems of intelligent persuasion that increasingly direct our thoughts and actions. As digital technologies have made information abundant, our attention has become the scarce resource – and in the digital "attention economy," technologies compete to capture and exploit our mere attention, rather than supporting the true goals we have for our lives. For too long, we've minimized the resulting harms as "distractions" or minor annoyances. Ultimately, however, they undermine the integrity of the human will at both individual and collective levels. Liberating human attention from the forces of intelligent persuasion may therefore be the defining moral and political task of the Information Age. Drawing on insights from ancient Greece as well as Silicon Valley, Williams's thoughtful and impassioned analysis brings much needed clarity to one of the most pressing questions of our time.

This title is also available as Open Access.

Stand Out of Our Light

Freedom and Resistance in the
Attention Economy

JAMES WILLIAMS
University of Oxford

CAMBRIDGE
UNIVERSITY PRESS

CAMBRIDGE
UNIVERSITY PRESS

University Printing House, Cambridge CB2 8BS, United Kingdom

One Liberty Plaza, 20th Floor, New York, NY 10006, USA

477 Williamstown Road, Port Melbourne, VIC 3207, Australia

314-321, 3rd Floor, Plot 3, Splendor Forum, Jasola District Centre, New Delhi - 110025, India

79 Anson Road, #06-04/06, Singapore 079906

Cambridge University Press is part of the University of Cambridge.

It furthers the University's mission by disseminating knowledge in the pursuit of education, learning and research at the highest international levels of excellence.

www.cambridge.org
Information on this title: www.cambridge.org/9781108452991
DOI: 10.1017/9781108453004

First published 2018

A catalogue record for this publication is available from the British Library

ISBN 978-1-108-42909-2 Hardback
ISBN 978-1-108-45299-1 Paperback

Cambridge University Press has no responsibility for the persistence or accuracy of URLs for external or third-party internet websites referred to in this publication, and does not guarantee that any content on such websites is, or will remain, accurate or appropriate.

For Alexander

It is disgraceful to be unable to use our good things.

Aristotle, *Politics*

Contents

Preface

In order to do anything that matters, we must first be able to give attention to the things that matter. Doing so has never been easy, but lately it's become harder in new and surprising ways.

While we weren't watching, a next generation threat to human freedom materialized right in front of our noses. We didn't notice it because it came in forms that were already familiar to us. It came bearing gifts of information, historically a scarce and valuable resource, but delivered them in such abundance, and with such velocity, that these gifts became a mountain of burdens. Most disarming of all, it came to us with the promise that it was *on our side*: that it was designed to help us navigate our lives in the ways *we* want them to go.

Yet these little wondrous machines, for all their potential, have not been entirely on our side. Rather than supporting our *intentions*, they have largely sought to grab and keep our *attention*. In their cutthroat competition against one another for the increasingly scarce prize of "persuading" us – of shaping our thoughts and actions in accordance with their predefined goals – they have been forced to resort to the cheapest, pettiest tricks in the book, appealing to the lowest parts of us, to the lesser selves that our higher natures perennially struggle to overcome. Furthermore, they now deploy in the service of this attentional capture and exploitation the most intelligent systems of computation the world has ever seen.

For too long, we've minimized the threats of this intelligent, adversarial persuasion as mere "distraction," or minor annoyance. In the short term, these challenges can indeed frustrate our ability to do the things we want to do. In the longer term, however, they can make it harder for us to live the lives we want to live, or, even worse, undermine fundamental capacities such as reflection and self-regulation, making it harder, in the words of philosopher Harry Frankfurt, to "want what we want to want." Seen in this light, these new attentional adversaries threaten not only the success but even the integrity of the human will, at both individual and collective levels.

Some threats to freedom we recognize immediately; others take time to reveal themselves for what they are. In the case of this intelligent, adversarial persuasion that increasingly pervades human life, the process of recognition is only beginning. The threats, by contrast – the infrastructures and incentives that underlie their operation – are now quite mature and deeply entrenched. As a result, it may be too late to bring these adversarial systems onto our side. They may now be too embedded in our lives to extricate. I do not believe this to be the case myself – the situation is not entirely hopeless – but the gate to salvation is narrow, and closing quickly.

I used to think there were no great political struggles left. The truly epic defenses of freedom, I thought, had already been fought and won by generations greater than my own, leaving to my time only the task of dutifully administering our hard-earned political inheritance.

How wrong I was. The liberation of human attention may be the defining moral and political struggle of our time. Its success is prerequisite for the success of virtually all other struggles. We therefore have an obligation to rewire this system of intelligent, adversarial persuasion before it rewires us. Doing so requires hacking together new ways of talking and thinking about the problem, as well as summoning the courage necessary for advancing on it in inconvenient and unpopular ways.

In the short space of this book, my aim is to calibrate the compass for this effort rather than draw up any detailed maps. I'll have more questions than answers; this will be more exploration than argument. Read this as an unfolding of intuitions, a quest for the right words. Ralph Waldo Emerson wrote, "sometimes a scream is better than a thesis." This will be a bit of both.

The brief, yet full, time during which I have written this book would not have been possible without the extraordinary generosity and foresight of the Kadas Prize Foundation, Cambridge University Press, the Centre for Research in the Arts, Social Sciences and Humanities (CRASSH) at the University of Cambridge, and the superhuman efforts of the Nine Dots Prize staff and board. This privilege is only compounded by the fact that it serves to inaugurate what will no doubt be a series of similar efforts to come. My hope is that the present effort proves worthy of the generosity of their, and your, attention.

I   Philosophy for Trolls

It was a bright warm morning in Corinth in the fourth-century BC, and everything seemed normal in the market. Shoppers eyeballed the wares of craftsmen and fishmongers. Sweat and the odour of feet gave the sea wind a sour smell. Birds cawed, waves lapped. Dogs followed each other into those places humans do not go. The day was proving to be plain in every way – until, all at once, a howl of Greek voices went up in a shared cry of anger and disgust. An empty circle formed in the crowd as shoppers began scooting back from something, or someone. It was a beggar, lying on the ground, reclining slightly against a big ceramic barrel he had apparently taken as his home. He wore only a loincloth, which he had, without announcement or concern, pulled aside as he began to pleasure himself in full view of the unfortunate patrons, who were by now shuffling away. But anyone who knew the man's identity was probably unsurprised by his act, perhaps even amused. This was no mere homeless man: this was Diogenes of Sinope, one of the most famous philosophers in all of Greece.

Most philosophers do not live in big ceramic barrels. But Diogenes was not an ordinary philosopher, and he did not intend to become one. Though he may never have written a single word of philosophy, tales of his life and knowledge of his views spread far and wide. He had no tribe or family of his own, having been exiled from his hometown for defacing currency. Diogenes had taken a vow of poverty (hence his residence in that big ceramic barrel), and spent much of his free time – which was, of course, *all* the time – heckling and spitting at passers-by, giving lectures to his dogs, and, of course, regaling his fellow citizens with public displays of onanism. He would often walk around with a lit lantern during the day, and when people would ask what he was doing, he would say, "I'm looking for an honest man." When asked what he thought was the most beautiful thing in the world, Diogenes replied, "Freedom of speech." At the same time, it's said that he attended lectures by other luminaries of the age, including Plato, just to disrupt them by eating loudly. He was notorious for being offensive, impulsive, and downright rude. Diogenes' presence was not a safe space. Today, we would no doubt call him a "troll."

Yet despite his notoriety, or perhaps because of it, he caught the attention of a very powerful man: Alexander the Great, arguably the most powerful person in the world at the time. In fact, Alexander so admired this Greek oddity, this famed philosopher-troll, that he's reported to have said, "If I were not Alexander, I should wish to be Diogenes."[1]

One day, Alexander finally paid Diogenes a visit. On the day in question, Diogenes was sunning himself in the grounds of the Craneum, a gymnasium in Corinth. Alexander approached Diogenes, flanked by what must have been an imposing retinue of bodyguards, servants, and soldiers, and fawningly expressed his admiration for this pitiful-looking homeless man wearing only a loincloth, lying on the ground before him. Then – perhaps it was on impulse, or perhaps it was by design – Alexander made Diogenes a remarkable offer: he promised to grant him any wish he desired. All Diogenes had to do was name it, and it would be done.

The air must have been thick with anticipation. How would Diogenes respond? Any offer, even a very good one, imposes an obligation on the person receiving it. This includes, at minimum, an obligation to perform one's gratefulness for having been offered anything at all, even if the offer is ultimately declined. However, even though he was a beggar, Diogenes was not really the grateful type. How, then, would he reply? Would he finally drop his trollish persona in the face of this life-changing offer? Would Diogenes ask Alexander to annul his exile from Sinope so he could return to his hometown after all these years? Or might he decline to consider Alexander's offer at all? Would the cranky philosopher-troll even bother to respond?

But Diogenes did respond. He looked up, gestured at Alexander, and barked, "Stand out of my light!"[2]

At the dawn of the twenty-first century, a new set of wondrous, designed forces – our information and communication technologies – has transformed human life. Our moment-to-moment experiences, our interactions with one another, the styles of our thoughts and the habits of our days now take their shapes, in large part, from the operation of these new inventions. Their inner workings are, for many of us, sufficiently obscure that they seem indistinguishable from magic; we are happy to be astonished by their novelty and power. And with our admiration comes a trust; that these inventions are, as their creators claim, built to follow *our* guiding lights, to help us navigate our lives in the ways *we* want them to go. We trust these wondrous inventions to be *on our side*.

In Alexander's offer to Diogenes we can detect a certain imperial optimism that is familiar to us from the way these young powers of our time, our digital Alexanders, have similarly come into our lives and offered to fulfill all manner of needs and wishes. Of course, in many ways they *have* fulfilled our needs and wishes, and in many ways they *have* been on our side. They have profoundly enhanced our ability to inform ourselves, to communicate with one another, and to understand our world. Today, with a thin plastic slab the size of my hand, I can chat with my family in Seattle, instantly read any Shakespeare play, or fire off a message to my elected representatives, regardless of where in the world I am.

And yet, as these new powers have become ever more central to our thought and action, we've begun to realize that they, like Alexander to Diogenes, have also been standing in our light, in a sense – and in one light in particular: a light so precious and central to human flourishing that without it all their other benefits may do us little good.

That light is the light of our attention. Something deep and potentially irreversible seems to be happening to human attention in the age of information. Responding to it well may be the biggest moral and political challenge of our time. My purpose here is to tell you why I think so – and to ask for your help in keeping this light lit.

NOTES

1 Diogenes Laertius vi. 32; Arrian VII.2.
2 Diogenes Laertius vi. 38; Arrian VII.2.

I   Distraction by Design

2   The Faulty GPS

Five years ago I was working for Google and advancing a mission that I still admire for its audacity of scope: "to organize the world's information and make it universally accessible and useful."[1] But one day I had an epiphany: there was more technology in my life than ever before, but it felt *harder* than ever to do the things I wanted to do.

I felt … *distracted*. But it was more than just "distraction" – this was some new mode of *deep* distraction I didn't have words for. Something was shifting on a level deeper than mere annoyance, and its disruptive effects felt far more perilous than the usual surface-level static we expect from day-to-day life. It felt like something disintegrating, decohering: as though the floor was crumbling under my feet, and my body was just beginning to realize it was falling. I felt the story of my life being compromised in some fuzzy way I couldn't articulate. The matter of my world seemed to be sublimating into thin air. Does that even make sense? It didn't at the time.

Whatever it was, this deep distraction seemed to have the exact opposite effect of the one technology is supposed to have on our lives. More and more, I found myself asking the question, "What was all this technology supposed to be *doing* for me?"

Think for a moment about the goals you have for yourself: your goals for reading this book, for later today, for this week, even for later this year and beyond. If you're like most people, they're probably goals like "learn how to play piano," "spend more time with family," "plan that trip I've been meaning to take," and so on. These are real goals, human goals. They're the kinds of goals that, when we're on our deathbeds, we'll regret not having achieved. If technology is *for* anything, it's for helping us pursue these kinds of goals.

A few years ago I read an article called "Regrets of the Dying."[2] It was about a businesswoman whose disillusionment with the day-to-day slog of her trade had led her to leave it, and to start working in a very different place: in rooms where people were dying. She spent her days attending to their needs and listening to their regrets, and she recorded the most common things they wished they'd done, or hadn't done, in life: they'd worked too hard, they hadn't told people how they felt, they hadn't let themselves be happy, and so on. This, it seems to me, is the proper perspective – the one that's truly our own, if any really is. It's the perspective that our screens and machines ought to help us circle back on, again and again: because whatever we might choose to want, nobody chooses to want to regret.

Think back on your goals from a moment ago. Now try to imagine what your technologies' goals are for you. What do you think *they* are? I don't mean the companies' mission statements and high-flying marketing messages – I mean the goals on the dashboards in their product design meetings, the metrics they're using to define what success means for your life. How likely do you think it is that they reflect the goals you have for yourself?

Not very likely, sorry to say. Instead of your goals, success from their perspective is usually defined in the form of low-level "engagement" goals, as they're often called. These include things like maximizing the amount of time you spend with their product, keeping you clicking or tapping or scrolling as much as possible, or showing you as many pages or ads as they can. A peculiar quirk of the technology industry is its ability to drain words of their deeper meanings; "engagement" is one such word. (Incidentally, it's fitting that this term can also refer to clashes between armies: here, the "engagement" is fundamentally adversarial as well.)

But these "engagement" goals are petty, subhuman goals. No person has these goals for themselves. No one wakes up in the morning and asks, "How much time can I possibly spend using social media today?" (If there is someone like that, I'd love to meet them and understand their mind.)

What this means, though, is that there's a deep misalignment between the goals we have for ourselves and the goals our technologies have for us. This seems to me to be a really big deal, and one that nobody talks about nearly enough. We trust these technologies to be companion systems for our lives: we trust them to help us do the things we want to do, to become the people we want to be.

In a sense, our information technologies ought to be GPSes for our lives. (Sure, there are times when we don't know *exactly* where we want to go in life. But in those cases, technology's job is to help us figure out what our destination is, and to do so in the way we *want* to figure it out.) But imagine if your *actual* GPS was adversarial against you in this way. Imagine that you've just purchased a new one, installed it in your car, and on the first use it guides you efficiently to the right place. On the second trip, however, it takes you to an address several streets away from your intended destination. It's probably just a random glitch, you think, or maybe it needs a map update. So you give it little thought. But on the third trip, you're shocked when you find yourself *miles* away from your desired endpoint, which is now on the opposite side of town. These errors continue to mount, and they frustrate you so much that you give up and decide to return home. But then, when you enter your home address, the system gives you a route that would have you drive for *hours* and end up in a totally different city.

Any reasonable person would consider this GPS faulty and return it to the store, if not chuck it out their car window. Who would continue to put up with a device they *knew* would take them somewhere other than where they wanted to go? What reasons could anyone possibly have for continuing to tolerate such a thing?

No one would put up with this sort of distraction from a technology that directs them through *physical* space. Yet we do precisely this, on a daily basis, when it comes to the technologies that direct us through *informational* space. We have a curiously high tolerance for poor navigability when it comes to the GPSes for our lives – the information and communication systems that now direct so much of our thought and action.

When I looked around the technology industry, I began to see with new eyes the dashboards, the metrics, and the goals that were driving much of its design. *These* were the destinations we were entering into the GPSes guiding the lives of millions of human beings. I tried imagining *my* life reflected in the primary color numbers incrementing on screens around me: Number of Views, Time on Site, Number of Clicks, Total Conversions. Suddenly, these goals seemed petty and perverse. They were not *my* goals – or anyone else's.

I soon came to understand that the cause in which I'd been conscripted wasn't the organization of *information* at all, but of *attention*. The technology industry wasn't designing products; it was designing users. These magical, general-purpose systems weren't neutral "tools"; they were purpose-driven navigation systems guiding the lives of flesh-and-blood humans. They were extensions of our attention. The Canadian media theorist Harold Innis once said that his entire career's work proceeded from the question, "Why do we attend to the things to which we attend?"[3] I realized that I'd been woefully negligent in asking this question about my own attention.

But I also knew this wasn't just about *me* – my deep distractions, my frustrated goals. Because when most people in society use your product, you aren't just designing users; you're designing society. But if all of society were to become as distracted in this new, deep way as I was starting to feel, what would that mean? What would be the implications for our shared interests, our common purposes, our collective identities, our politics?

In 1985 the educator and media critic Neil Postman wrote *Amusing Ourselves to Death*, a book that's become more relevant and prescient with each passing day.[4] In its foreword, Postman recalls Aldous Huxley's observation from *Brave New World Revisited* that the defenders of freedom in his time had "failed to take into account ... man's almost infinite appetite for distractions."[5] Postman contrasts the indirect, persuasive threats to human freedom that Huxley warns about in *Brave New World* with the direct, coercive sort of threats on which George Orwell focuses in *Nineteen Eighty-Four*.

Huxley's foresight, Postman writes, lay in his prediction that free-dom's nastiest adversaries in the years to come would emerge not from the things we fear, but from the things that give us pleasure: it's not the prospect of a "boot stamping on a human face – forever" that should keep us up at night, but rather the specter of a situation in which "people will come to love their oppression, to adore the tech-nologies that undo their capacities to think."[6] A thumb scrolling through an infinite feed, forever.

I wondered whether, in the design of digital technologies, we'd made the same mistake as Huxley's contemporaries: I wondered whether we'd failed to take into account our "almost infinite appetite for distractions." I didn't know the answer, but I felt the question required urgent, focused attention.

NOTES

1 Google (2017). Our Company. www.google.com/intl/en/about/our-company/
  Note: All the web pages referenced herein were accessed within the period November 1–December 31, 2017.
2 Ware, Bronnie (2009). Regrets of the Dying. www.bronnieware.com/blog/regrets-of-the-dying
3 Innis, Harold A. (2008). *The Bias of Communication*. University of Toronto Press.
4 Books I refer to often are included in the Further Reading list at the end of this book.
5 Huxley, Aldous (1985). *Brave New World Revisited*. New York, NY: Harper & Brothers.
6 Postman, Neil (1987). *Amusing Ourselves to Death*. Harmondsworth: Penguin.

3   The Age of Attention

To see what is in front of one's nose needs a constant struggle.

Orwell

When I told my mother I was moving to the other side of the planet to study technology ethics at a school that's almost three times as old as my country, she asked, "Why would you go somewhere so *old* to study something so *new*?" In a way, the question contained its own answer. Working in the technology industry, I felt, was akin to climbing a mountain, and that's one way – a very up-close and hands-on way – to get to know a mountain. But if you want to see its shape, paint its profile, understand its relations with the wider geography – to do that, you have to go a few miles away and look back. I felt that my inquiry into the faulty GPSes of my life required this move. I needed distance, not only physical but also temporal and ultimately critical, from the windy yet intriguing cliffs of the technology industry. "Amongst the rocks one cannot stop or think."[1] Sometimes, the struggle to see what's in front of your nose is a struggle to get away from it so you can see it as a whole.

I soon found that my quest to gain distance from the mountain of the technology industry was paralleling, and in many ways enabling, a more general quest to gain distance from the assumptions of the Information Age altogether. I suspect that no one living in a named age – the Bronze Age, the Iron Age – ever called it by the name we give it now. They no doubt used other names rooted in assumptions of their times that they could not imagine would ever be overturned. So it's always both bemused and annoyed me, in roughly equal measure, that we so triumphantly call our time the "Information Age." Information is the water in which we swim; we perceive it to be the raw material of the human experience. So the dominant metaphor for the human is now the computer, and we interpret the challenges of our world primarily in terms of the management of information.

This is, of course, the standard way people talk about digital technologies: it's assumed that *information* is fundamentally what they're managing, manipulating, and moving around. For example, ten seconds before I started writing this sentence my wife walked into the room and said, "I just heard the internet described on the radio as 'a conveyor belt of fraudulent information.'" Every day, we hear dozens of remarks like this: on the radio, in the newspaper, and in conversations with others. We instinctively frame issues pertaining to digital technologies in informational terms, which means that the political and ethical challenges we end up worrying about most of the time also involve the management of information: privacy, security, surveillance, and so on.

This is understandable. For most of human history, we've lived in environments of information scarcity. In those contexts, the implicit goal of information technologies has been to *break down* the barriers between us and information. Because information was scarce, any new piece of it represented a novel addition to your life. You had plenty of capacity to attend to it and integrate it into your general picture of the world. For example, a hundred years ago you could stand on a street corner in a city and start preaching, and people would probably stop and listen. They had the time and attention to spare. And because information has historically been scarce, the received wisdom has been that more information is better. The advent of digital computing, however, broke down the barriers between us and information to an unprecedented degree.

Yet, as the noted economist Herbert Simon pointed out in the 1970s, when information becomes abundant, *attention* becomes the scarce resource:

> in an information-rich world, the wealth of information means a dearth of something else: a scarcity of whatever it is that

information consumes. What information consumes is rather obvious: it consumes the attention of its recipients. Hence a wealth of information creates a poverty of attention and a need to allocate that attention efficiently among the overabundance of information sources that might consume it.[2]

Since Simon's time, the ubiquity of small, constantly connected, general-purpose computers has produced this information–attention inversion on a global scale. Today you can access most any piece of information, or contact most anyone you wish, via a small device in your pocket not much bigger than a cigarette box. This capacity for instantaneous information and connection has come to form the background of our experience astonishingly quickly. That is to say, our informational *tools* have rapidly become our informational *environment*. What's more, predigital media such as television and radio have largely been digitally retrofitted, rendering the networked digital environment a constant presence in human life. Today, in the average household in North America, you will find thirteen internet-connected devices.[3]

This inversion between information and attention has so completely pervaded our lives that it's now (perhaps paradoxically) harder for us to notice its effects. There seems to have been a period around the time the field of cybernetics, or the science of control systems, was emerging, when it was easier to recognize the nature of this shift. This is the period in which Simon was writing, and when the Canadian media theorist Marshall McLuhan and others were beginning to put the concept of "media ecology" on the radar of popular culture.[4] Now, however, we've pretty much lost all touch with any perceptual benchmarks against which we might judge how utterly our information technologies have enveloped our lives. We get fragmentary glimpses of that old world from time to time: when we go camping, when we take a long flight without internet connectivity, when our phone dies for several days, or when we intentionally take a digital "detox." But these increasingly rare occurrences are exceptions, not the rule. Barring some unthinkable global catastrophe, the old world of information scarcity seems to be gone for good.

But what does it *really* mean to say that information abundance produces attention scarcity? Abundance can only be abundant relative to some threshold, so we might ask, "What is information now abundant relative to?" One answer would be "The amount of information available historically." While true, this doesn't seem like the *really* relevant threshold we should be interested in. For our purposes, we're only incidentally concerned with the *historical* story here: the mere increase in information between two time points isn't, in itself, a problem. Rather, the relevant threshold seems to be a *functional* one: what matters to us is whether the amount of information is above or below the threshold of what can be well processed given existing limitations.

To illustrate what I mean, consider the video game *Tetris*. The goal of *Tetris* is to rotate, stack, and clear different configurations of blocks as they rain down one by one from off screen, which they do at a constantly increasing rate of speed. The total number of bricks waiting off screen for you to stack is infinite – the game can keep going for as long as you can – but their infinitude, their abundance, is not the problem. The challenge of the game, and what ultimately does you in, is the increasing speed at which they fall. In the same way, information quantity *as such* is only important insofar as it enables information velocity. At extreme speeds, processing fails.

So the main risk information abundance poses is not that one's attention will be *occupied* or *used up* by information, as though it were some finite, quantifiable resource, but rather that one will *lose control over* one's attentional processes. In other words, the problems in *Tetris* arise not when you stack a brick in the wrong place (though this can contribute to problems down the line), but rather when you lose control of the ability to direct, rotate, and stack the bricks altogether.

It's precisely in this area – the keeping or losing of control – where the personal and political challenges of information abundance, and attention scarcity, arise. To say that information abundance produces attention scarcity means that the problems we encounter are now less about breaking down barriers between us and information, and more about putting barriers in place. It means that the really important sort of censorship we ought to worry about pertains less to the management of information, and more to the management of attention.

Here's the problem: Many of the systems we've developed to help guide our lives – systems like news, education, law, advertising, and so on – arose in, and still assume, an environment of information scarcity. We're only just beginning to explore what these systems should do for us, and how they need to change, in this new milieu of information abundance.

We call our time the Information Age, but I think a better name for it would be the "Age of Attention." In the Age of Attention, digital technologies are uniquely poised to help us grapple with the new challenges we face – challenges which are, fundamentally, challenges of self-regulation.

NOTES

1 Eliot, T. S. (1922). *The Waste Land*. New York, NY: Boni & Liveright.
2 Simon, Herbert A. (1971). Designing Organizations for an Information-Rich World. *Computers, Communication, and the Public Interest* (pp. 40–41). Baltimore, MD: Johns Hopkins University Press.
3 Fanelli, Matthew (2017). Getting Consumers' Attention Across Every Screen They have at Home. eMarketer, December 5. www.emarketer.com/Article/Getting-Consumers-Attention-Across-Every-Screen-They-Have-Home/1016798
4 McLuhan, Marshall (1964). *Understanding Media*. New York, NY: Mentor. Postman, Neil (1970). The Reformed English Curriculum. *High School 1980: The Shape of the Future in American Secondary Education*, ed. A.C. Eurich. London: Pitman.

4   Bring your own Boundaries

Who will be great, must be able to limit himself.

Goethe

I mostly grew up in west Texas, in a town called Abilene, which is big enough that you might have heard it in country songs, where it rhymes with names like Eileen or Darlene, or phrases like "treat you mean" or "I ever seen," but it's still small enough that when I was in high school Microsoft Word would autocorrect its name to "abalone," which refers to a species of marine snail with a shell that's tough and cloddish on the outside, but slippery and rainbow-like within, as though someone had tried to flush out the little being inside with gasoline.

In my senior year of high school in Abilene I signed up for calculus, a class that required me to have a graphing calculator – one of those bigger models, with a dot-matrix display that lets you visualize the implications of your equations when they get too complex to imagine in your head, or to work out easily on paper. So I acquired a Texas Instruments TI-83, the latest model, which had come out just a couple of years earlier. An older model would have sufficed, but the TI-83 had native support for something called assembly programming languages, which meant you could load programs onto it that did *anything*, not just graph equations. This meant that practically, it wasn't just a "calculator" anymore; it was a full-fledged, "general-purpose" computer. One of my classmates found a program somewhere for the game *Tetris*, and soon enough I had that loaded onto my calculator too. When class got boring, I'd sometimes load the *Tetris* program and play it to pass the time. Before long, I found myself realizing I'd opened the game and started playing it automatically, without consciously deciding to do so. It was just so convenient, having *fun* waiting a few key-clicks away – and it was usually far more rewarding than listening to the teacher drone on about integrals and differentials. That is to say, it was more *immediately* rewarding – right then, in that moment.

Soon, I started falling behind in class. Distracted by calculator-*Tetris*, my grades began to slide. This wasn't anyone else's fault, of course; *I* had loaded the program onto my calculator, and *I* was the one who kept opening and playing the game. But I didn't want to tell anyone about the problem because I was embarrassed and ashamed to have let myself get derailed by so trivial a thing. I kept putting off my day of reckoning with this distraction, and its effects continued to mount. I carried my constant knowledge of the problem with me, as well as my failure to look it in the face, which made me turn to the quick pleasures of its immediate rewards even more. I hated how impulsive and weak of will I had become, but I kept turning again to the very cause of it to find a consolation that I knew was fleeting and illusory. The bricks kept falling quicker. I kept misstacking them. The pile kept getting higher. The music kept getting faster.

The "game over" moment finally came on a school trip in a nearby town, where I had been scheduled to participate in a journalism competition. At the last minute, word had come through from my school that I was no longer eligible to compete because I had failed my last calculus test. I had never failed a test in my life.

If you wanted to train all of society to be as impulsive and weak-willed as possible, how would you do it? One way would be to invent an impulsivity training device – let's call it an iTrainer – that delivers an endless supply of informational rewards on demand. You'd want to make it small enough to fit in a pocket or purse so people could carry it anywhere they went. The informational rewards it would pipe into their attentional world could be anything, from cute cat photos to tidbits of news that outrage you (because outrage can, after all, be a reward too). To boost its effectiveness, you could endow the iTrainer with rich systems of intelligence and automation so it could adapt to users' behaviors, contexts, and individual quirks in order to get them to spend as much time and attention with it as possible.

So let's say you build the iTrainer and distribute it gradually into society. At first, people's willpower would probably be pretty strong and resistant. The iTrainer might also cause some awkward social situations, at least until enough people had adopted it that it was widely accepted, and not seen as weird. But if everyone were to keep using it over several years, you'd probably start seeing it work pretty well. Now, the iTrainer might make people's lives harder to live, of course; it would no doubt get in the way of them pursuing their desired tasks and goals. Even though you created it, you probably wouldn't let your kids use one. But from the point of view of *your* design goals – in other words, making the world more impulsive and weak-willed – it would likely be a roaring success.

Then, what if you wanted to take things even further? What if you wanted to make everyone even *more* distracted, angry, cynical – and even unsure of what, or how, to think? What if you wanted to troll everyone's minds? You'd probably create an engine, a set of economic incentives, that would make it profitable for other people to produce and deliver these rewards – and, where possible, you'd make these the *only* incentives for doing so. You don't want just any rewards to get delivered – you want people to receive rewards that speak to their impulsive selves, rewards that are the best at punching the right buttons in their brains. For good measure, you could also centralize the ownership of this design as much as possible.

If you'd done all this ten years ago, right about now you'd probably be seeing some interesting results. You'd probably see nine out of ten people never leaving home without their iTrainer.[1] Almost half its users would say they couldn't even *live* without their device.[2] You'd probably see them using it to access most of the information they consume, across every context of life, from politics to education to celebrity gossip and beyond. You'd probably find they were using the iTrainer hundreds of times per day, spending a third of their waking lives engaged with it, and it would probably be the first and last thing they engaged with every day.[3]

If you wanted to train society to be as weak-willed and impulsive as possible, you could do a whole lot worse than this. In any event, after unleashing the iTrainer on the world, it would be absurd to claim that it hadn't produced significant changes in the thoughts, behaviors, and habits of its users. After all, everyone would have been part of a rigorous impulsivity training program for many years! What's more, this program would have effectively done an end run around many of our other societal systems; it would have opened a door directly onto our attentional capacities, and become a lens through which society sees the world. It would, of course, be a major undertaking to try to understand the full story about what effects this project had had in people's lives – not only as individuals, but also for society as a whole. It would certainly have had major implications for the way we had been collectively discussing and deciding questions of great importance. And it would certainly have given us, as did previous forms of media, political candidates that were made in its image.

Of course, the iTrainer project would never come anywhere close to passing a research ethics review. Launching such a project of societal reshaping, and letting it run unchecked, would clearly be utterly outrageous. So it's a good thing this is all just a thought experiment.

The new challenges we face in the Age of Attention are, on both individual and collective levels, challenges of self-regulation. Having *some* limits is inevitable in human life. In fact, limits are necessary if we are to have any freedom at all. As the American philosopher Harry Frankfurt puts it: "What has no boundaries has no shape."[4] Reason, relationships, racetracks, rules of games, sunglasses, walls of buildings, lines on a page: our lives are full of useful constraints to which we freely submit so that we can achieve otherwise unachievable ends. "To be driven by our appetites alone is slavery," wrote Rousseau in

The Social Contract, "while to obey a law that we have imposed on ourselves is freedom" (p. 59). Even our old friend Diogenes, lover of unrestrained living that he was, said, "for the conduct of life we need right reason or a halter."[5] When we apply restraints upon ourselves that channel our activities toward our higher goals – some call these restraints "commitment devices" – we reach heights that would have been otherwise unreachable. If Odysseus had not instructed his sailors to tie him to the mast (and to plug up their own ears with wax), he would never have heard the sirens' song and lived to tell about it.

For most of human history, when you were born you inherited an off-the-shelf package of religious and cultural constraints. This was a kind of library of limits that was embedded in your social and physical environment. These limits performed certain self-regulatory tasks for you so you didn't have to take them on yourself. The packages included habits, practices, rituals, social conventions, moral codes, and a myriad of other constraints that had typically evolved over many centuries, if not millennia, to reliably guide – or shall we say *design* – our lives in the direction of particular values, and to help us give attention to the things that matter most.

In the twentieth century the rise of secularism and modernism in the West occasioned the collapse – if not the jettisoning – of many of these off-the-shelf packages of constraints in the cause of the liberation of the individual. In many cases, this rejection occurred on the basis of philosophical or cosmological disagreements with the old packages. This has, of course, had many great benefits. Yet by rejecting entire packages of constraint, we've also rejected those constraints that *were* actually useful for our purposes. "The left's project of liberation," writes the American philosopher Matthew Crawford, "led us to dismantle inherited cultural jigs that once imposed a certain coherence (for better and worse) on individual lives. This created a vacuum of cultural authority that has been filled, opportunistically, with attentional landscapes that get installed by whatever 'choice architect' brings the most energy to the task – usually because it sees the profit potential." The German philosopher Peter Sloterdijk, in his book *You Must Change Your Life,* has called for a reclamation of this particular aspect of religion – its habits and practices – which he calls "anthropotechnics."[6]

When you dismantle existing boundaries in your environment, it frees you from their limitations, but it requires you to bring your *own* boundaries where you didn't have to before. Sometimes, taking on this additional self-regulatory burden is totally worth it. Other times, though, the cost is too high. According to the so-called "ego-depletion" hypothesis, our self-control, our willpower, is a finite resource.[7] So when the self-regulatory cost of bringing your own boundaries is high enough, it takes away willpower that could have been spent on something else.

This increase in self-regulatory burden may pose a unique challenge for those living in poverty, who, research suggests are more likely to begin from a place of willpower depletion relative to everyone else. This is largely due to the many decisions and trade-offs they must make on a day-to-day basis that those who don't live in poverty don't have to make.[8] Diogenes once said that "disabled" ought to mean "poor," and to the extent that living in poverty means one's willpower can be more easily depleted, he was more right than he knew.[9] But the wider implication here is that these problems of self-regulation in the face of information abundance aren't just "first-world problems." They carry large implications for the societal goals of justice and equality. If the first "digital divide" disenfranchised those who couldn't access information, today's digital divide disenfranchises those who can't pay attention.[10]

It's against this cultural backdrop, of having to bring our own boundaries where we didn't before, that digital technologies have posed these new challenges of self-regulation. Like the iTrainer in my thought experiment, digital technologies have transformed our experiential world into a never-ending flow of potential informational rewards. They've become the playing field on which everything now competes for our attention. Similar to economic abundance, "if these rewards arrive faster than the disciplines of prudence can form, then self-control will *decline* with affluence: the affluent (with everyone else) will become less prudent."[11] In a sense, information abundance requires us to invert our understanding of what "information technologies" do: Rather than overcoming barriers in the world, they increasingly exist to help us put barriers in place. The headphone manufacturer Bose now sells a product called Hearphones that allows the user to block out all sounds in their environment except the ones coming from their desired source – to focus on a conversation in a loud room, for example. The product's website reads: "Focus on the voices you want to hear – and filter out the noises you don't – so you can comfortably hear every word. From now on, how you hear is up to you."[12] We could also read this tagline as a fitting description of the new challenges in the Age of Attention as a whole.

The increasing rate of technological change further amplifies these challenges of attention and self-regulation. Historically, new forms of media took years, if not generations, to be adopted, analyzed, and adapted to. Today, however, new technologies can arrive on the scene and rapidly scale to millions of users in the course of months or even days. The constant stream of new products this unleashes – along with the ongoing optimization of features within products already in use – can result in a situation in which users are in a constant state of learning and adaptation to new interaction dynamics, familiar enough with their technologies to operate them, but never so fully in control that they can prevent the technologies from operating on *them* in unexpected or undesirable ways. This keeps us living on what I sometimes call a "treadmill of incompetence."

In his essay "Reflections on Progress", Aldous Huxley writes, "however powerful and well trained the surface will is, it is not a match for circumstances."[13] Indeed, one of the major lessons of the past several decades of psychology research has been the power of people's environments in shaping their thoughts and behaviors. On one level, these effects may be temporary, such as changes in one's mood. As Nikola Tesla observed, "One may feel a sudden wave of sadness and rake his brain for an explanation when he might have noticed that it was caused by a cloud cutting off the rays of the sun."[14] Yet our environments can also have deep, long-lasting influences on our underlying capacities – even how autonomous (or nonautonomous) we are able to be. The Oxford philosopher Neil Levy writes in his book *Neuroethics*, "Autonomy is *developmentally* dependent upon the environment: we become autonomous individuals, able to control our behavior in the light of our values, only if the environment in which we grow up is suitably structured to reward self-control."[15]

Yet in the absence of environments that reward self-control or provide effective commitment devices, we're left to our *own* devices – and given our inherent scarcity of attention, the resulting cognitive overload often makes bringing our own boundaries extremely challenging, if not prohibitive. Limiting our lives in the right way was already hard enough, but in the Age of Attention we encounter even stronger headwinds. Of course, digital technology is uniquely poised to help us deal with these new challenges. And if technology exists to solve problems in our lives, it *ought* to help us surmount these challenges.

Unfortunately, far from helping us mitigate these challenges of self-regulation, our technologies have largely been amplifying them. Rather than helping us to more effectively stack and clear the *Tetris* bricks in our lives, they've been making the blocks fall faster than we ever imagined they could.

NOTES

1 Deutsche Telekom AG (2012). Smart Payments – How the Cell Phone Becomes a Wallet. www.studie-life.de/en/life-reports/smart-payments/
2 Smith, Aaron (2015). U.S. Smartphone Use in 2015. Pew Research Center. www.pewinternet.org/2015/04/01/us-smartphone-use-in-2015/
3 Perlow, Leslie A. (2012). *Sleeping with Your Smartphone: How to Break the 24/7 Habit and Change the Way you Work*. Boston, MA: Harvard Business Review Press. Andrews, S., Ellis, D. A., Shaw, H. and Piwek, L. (2015). Beyond Self-Report: Tools to Compare Estimated and Real-World Smart-phone Use. *PLoS One*, 10 (10), 1–9. dscout (2016). Mobile

Touches: dscout's Inaugural Study on Humans and their Tech. https://
blog.dscout.com/hubfs/downloads/dscout_mobile_touches_study_
2016.pdf

4 Frankfurt, Harry G. (1988). *The Importance of What We Care About:
Philosophical Essays*. Cambridge University Press.

5 Diogenes Laertius vi. 24; Arrian VII.2.

6 Sloterdijk, P. (2014). *You Must Change Your Life*. Hoboken, NJ: John
Wiley.

7 Baumeister, R. F., Bratslavsky, E., Muraven, M. and Tice, D. M. (1998). Ego
Depletion: Is the Active Self a Limited Resource? *Journal of Personality
and Social Psychology*, 74 (5), 1252–1265. https://doi.org/10.1037/0022-
3514.74.5.1252

8 Banerjee, Abhijit and Mullainathan, Sendhil (2010). The Shape of
Temptation: Implications for the Economic Lives of the Poor. National
Bureau of Economic Research working paper. www.nber.org/papers/
w15973. Spears, Dean (2010). Economic Decision-making in Poverty
Depletes Behavioral Control. Centre for Economic Policy Studies, working
paper. www.princeton.edu/ceps/workingpapers/213spears.pdf. Vohs, K.
D., Baumeister, R. F., Schmeichel, B. J., Twenge, J. M., Nelson, N. M., Tice,
D. M. and Cirino, K. (2008). Making Choices Impairs Subsequent
Self-Control: A Limited-Resource Account of Decision Making,
Self-Regulation, and Active Initiative. *Journal of Personality and Social
Psychology*, 94 (5), 883–898. https://doi.org/10.1037/0022-3514.94.5.883

9 Diogenes Laertius vi. 33; Arrian VII.2.

10 Norris, Pippa (2001). *Digital Divide: Civic Engagement, Information
Poverty, and the Internet Worldwide*. Cambridge University Press.

11 Offer, Avner (2006). *The Challenge of Affluence: Self-Control and
Well-being in the United States and Britain Since 1950*. Oxford
University Press.

12 Bose (2017). Bose HearPhones. www.bose.com/en_us/products/
headphones/conversation_enhancing_headphones/hearphones.html

13 Huxley, Aldous and Smith, Huston (2013). *The Divine Within: Selected
Writings on Enlightenment*. New York, NY: Harper Perennial.

14 Tesla, Nikola (1919). *My Inventions*, p. 56.

15 Levy, Neil (2007). *Neuroethics*. Cambridge University Press, p. xxx.

5   Empires of the Mind

The empires of the future are the empires of the mind.

Churchill

There was once a man walking down a road, wearing a cloak to keep warm. The North Wind noticed him and said to the Sun, "Let's see which one of us can get that man to take off his cloak. I bet I'll surely win, for no one can resist the gales of my mighty breath!" The Sun agreed to the contest, so the North Wind went first and started blowing at the man as hard as he could. The man's hat flew off; leaves swirled in the air all around him. He could barely take a step forward, but he clutched his cloak tightly – and no matter how hard the North Wind blew, the man's cloak stayed on. "What? Impossible!" the North Wind said. "Well, if *I* have failed," he said to the Sun, "then *surely* there is no hope for *you*." "We shall see," said the Sun. The Sun welled up his chest and made himself as bright as he could possibly be. The man, still walking, had to shield his eyes because the Sun's shine was so intense. Soon the man grew so warm inside his wool cloak that he began to feel faint: he started to stagger, sweat dripping off his head into the dirt. Breathing deeply, he untied his cloak and flung it over his shoulder, all the while scanning his environs for a source of water where he could cool off. The Sun's persuasion had won out where the North Wind's coercion could not.

This story comes from Aesop, the Greek fabulist who lived a few hundred years before Diogenes ever trolled the streets of Corinth. Like Diogenes, Aesop was also a slave at one point in his life before eventually being freed. Aesop died in Delphi, where the famous oracle lived upon whose temple was inscribed that famous maxim "Know Thyself." You probably know some of Aesop's other fables – "The Tortoise and the Hare," "The Ant and the Grasshopper," "The Dog and its Reflection" – but "The North Wind and the Sun" is one of my favorites, because it shows us that persuasion can be just as powerful, if not more so, than coercion.[1]

Of all the ways humans try to influence each other, persuasion might be the most prevalent and consequential. A marriage proposal. A car dealer's sales pitch. The temptation of Christ. A political stump speech. This book. When we consider the stories of our lives, and the stories that give our lives meaning, we find that they often turn on pivot points of persuasion. Since ancient Greece, persuasion has been understood primarily in its linguistic form, as *rhetorike techne*, or the art of the orator. Aristotle identified what he saw as three pillars of rhetoric – ethos, pathos, and logos – which roughly correspond to our notions of authority, emotion, and reason. And into medieval times, persuasion held a central position in education, alongside grammar and logic, as one-third of the classical trivium.

Yet *all* design is "persuasive" in a broad sense; it all directs our thoughts or actions in one way or another.[2] There's no such thing as a "neutral" technology. All design embodies certain goals and values; all design shapes the world in some way. A technology can no more be neutral than a government can be neutral. In fact, the *cyber-* in "cybernetics" and the *gover-* in "government" both stem from the same Greek root: *kyber-*, "to steer or to guide," originally used in the context of the navigation of ships. (This nautical metaphor provides a fitting illustration of what I mean: The idea of a "neutral" rudder is an incoherent one. Certainly, a rudder held straight can help you stay the course – but it won't guide your ship *somewhere*. Nor, in the same way, does any technology.)

However, some design is "persuasive" in a narrower sense than this. Some design has a form that follows directly from a specific representation of users' thoughts or behaviors, that the designer wants to change. This sort of persuasive design is by no means unique to digital technologies; humans have long designed physical environments toward such persuasive ends. Consider, for instance, the placement of escalators in shopping malls, the music in grocery stores, or

the layouts of cities.[3] Yet what Churchill said about physical architecture – "we shape our buildings, and afterwards, our buildings shape
us" – is just as true of the information architectures in which we now
spend so much of our lives.[4]

For most of human history, persuasive design in this narrower
sense has been a more or less handicraft undertaking. It's had the
character of an art rather than a science. As a result, we haven't
worried too much about its power over us. Instead, we've kept an
eye on coercive, as opposed to persuasive, designs. As Postman
pointed out, we've been more attuned to the Orwellian than the
Huxleyan threats to our freedom.

But now the winds have changed. While we weren't watching,
persuasion became industrialized. In the twentieth century the
modern advertising industry came to maturity and began systematically applying new knowledge about human psychology and decision
making. In parallel, advertising's scope expanded beyond the mere
provision of information to include the shaping of behaviors and
attitudes. By the end of the twentieth century, new forms of electric
media afforded advertisers new platforms and strategies for their persuasion, but the true effectiveness of their efforts was still hard to
measure. Then, the internet came along and closed the feedback loop
of measurement. Very quickly, an unprecedented infrastructure of
analytics, experimentation, message delivery, customization, and
automation emerged to enable digital advertising practices. Furthermore, networked general-purpose computers were becoming more
portable and connected, and people were spending more time than
ever with them. Designers began applying techniques and infrastructures developed for digital advertising to advance persuasive goals in
the platforms and services themselves. The scalability and increasing
profitability of digital advertising made it the default business model,
and thus incentive structure, for digital platforms and services. As a
result, goals and metrics that served the ends of advertising became
the dominant goals and metrics in the design of digital services themselves. By and large, these metrics involved capturing the maximum

amount of users' time and attention possible. In order to win the fierce global competition for our attention, design was forced to speak to the lowest parts of us, and to exploit our cognitive vulnerabilities.

This is how the twenty-first century began: with sophisticated persuasion allying with sophisticated technology to advance the pettiest possible goals in our lives. It began with the AI behind the system that beat the world champion at the board game Go recommending videos to keep me watching YouTube longer.[5]

There's no good analogue for this monopoly of the mind the forces of industrialized persuasion now hold – especially on the scale of *billions* of minds. Perhaps Christian adherents carrying the Bible everywhere they go, or the memorization of full Homeric epics in the Greek oral tradition, or the assignment of Buddhist mantras to recite all day under one's breath, or the total propaganda machines of totalitarian states. But we must look to the religious, the mythic, the totalistic, to find any remotely appropriate comparison. We have not been primed, either by nature or habit, to notice, much less struggle against, these new persuasive forces that so deeply shape our attention, our actions, and our lives.

This problem is not new just in scale, but also in kind. The empires of the *present* are the empires of the mind.

On October 26, 1994, if you had fired up your 28.8k modem, double-clicked the icon for the newly released Netscape Navigator web browser, and accessed the website of *Wired Magazine*, you would have seen a rectangle at the top of the page. In it, tie-dye text against a black background would have asked you, "Have you ever clicked your mouse right HERE? *You will.*"[6] Whether intended as prediction or command, this message – the first banner ad on the web – was more correct than its creators could have imagined. Digital ad spend was projected to pass $223 billion in 2017, and to continue to grow at double-digit rates until at least 2020.[7] Digital advertising is by far the dominant business model for monetizing information on the internet today. Many of the most widely used platforms, such as Google,

Facebook, and Twitter, are at core advertising companies. As a result, many of the world's top software engineers, designers, analysts, and statisticians now spend their days figuring out how to direct people's thinking and behavior toward predefined goals that may not align with their own. As Jeff Hammerbacher, Facebook's first research scientist, remarked: "The best minds of my generation are thinking about how to make people click ads ... and it sucks."[8]

As a media dynamic, advertising has historically been an *exception to the rule* of information delivery in a given medium. It's the newspaper ads, but not the articles; it's the billboards, but not the street signs; it's the TV commercials, but not the programs. In a world of information scarcity, it was useful to make these exceptions to the rule because they gave us novel information that could help us make better purchasing decisions. This has, broadly speaking, been the justification for advertising's existence in an information-scarce world.

In the mid twentieth century, as the modern advertising industry was coming to maturity, it started systematically applying new knowledge about human psychology and decision making. Psychologists such as Sigmund Freud had laid the groundwork for the study of unconscious thought, and in the 1970s Daniel Kahneman and Amos Tversky revealed the ways in which our automatic modes of thinking can override more rational rules of statistical prediction.[9] In fact a great deal of our everyday experience consists of such automatic, nonconscious processes; our lives take place, as the researchers John Bargh and Tanya Chartrand have said, against the backdrop of an "unbearable automaticity of being."[10] On the basis of all this new knowledge about human psychology and decision making, advertising's scope continued to expand beyond the informational to the persuasive; beyond shaping behaviors to shaping attitudes.[11] And new forms of electric media were giving them new avenues for their persuasion.

Yet most advertising remained faith-based. Without a comprehensive, reliable measurement infrastructure, it was impossible to study the effectiveness of one's advertising efforts, or to know how to improve on them. As John Wanamaker, a department store owner around the beginning of the twentieth century, is reported to have said, "Half the money I spend on advertising is wasted; the trouble is I don't know which half."[12] The potential for computing to revolutionize advertising measurement was recognized as early as the 1960s, when advertising agencies began experimenting with large mainframe computers. Companies such as Nielsen were also beginning to use diary and survey panel methods to understand audiences and their consumption behaviors, which marginally improved advertising intelligence by providing access to demographic data. However, these methods were laborious and expensive, and their aggregate data was useful only directionally. Measuring the actual effectiveness of ads was still largely infeasible.

The internet changed all that. Digital technology enabled a Cambrian explosion of advertising measurement. It was now possible to measure – at the level of individual users – people's behaviors (e.g. page views), intentions (e.g. search queries), contexts (e.g. physical locations), interests (e.g. inferences from users' browsing behavior), unique identifiers (e.g. device IDs or emails of logged-in users), and more. Also, vastly improved "benchmarking" data – information about the advertising efforts of one's competitors – became available via market intelligence services like comScore and Hitwise. Web browsers were key in enabling this sea change of advertising measurement, not only because of their new technical affordances, but also because of the precedent they set for subsequent measurement capabilities in other contexts.

In particular, the browser "cookie" – a small file delivered imperceptibly via website code to track user behavior across pages – played an essential role. In his book *The Daily You*, Joseph Turow writes that the cookie did "more to shape advertising – and social attention – on the web than any other invention apart from the browser itself."[13] Cookies are also emblematic, in their scope-creep, of digital advertising measurement as a whole. Initially, cookies were created to enable "shopping cart" functionality on retail websites; they were a way for the site to keep track of a user as he or she moved from page to page. Soon, however, they were being used to track people between sites, and indeed all across the web. Many groups raised privacy concerns about these scope-creeping cookies, and it soon became commonplace to speak of two main types: "first-party" cookies (cookies created by the site itself) and "third-party" cookies (cookies created by someone else). In 1997 the Internet Engineering Task Force proposed taking away third-party cookies, which sent the online advertising industry into a frenzy.[14] Ultimately, though, third-party cookies became commonplace. As unique identifiers at the level of the web-browser session, cookies paved the way for unique identifiers at higher levels, such as the device and even the user. Since 2014, for instance, Google's advertising platform has been able to track whether you visit a company's store in person after you see their ad.[15]

To manage this fire hose of measurement, "analytics" systems – such as Omniture, Coremetrics, and Google Analytics – emerged to serve as unified interfaces for managing one's advertising as well as nonadvertising data. In doing so, they helped establish the "engagement" metrics of advertising (e.g. number of clicks, impressions, or time on site) as default operational metrics for websites themselves. This effectively extended the design logic of advertising – and particularly *attention*-oriented advertising (as opposed to advertising that serves users' *intentions*) – to the design of the entire user experience.

In previous media, advertising had largely been an *exception* to the rule of information delivery – but in digital media, it seemed to have broken down some essential boundary; it seemed now to have *become* the rule. If advertising was previously said to be "underwriting" the dominant design goals of a medium, in digital media it now seemed to be "overwriting" them with its own. It wasn't just that the line between advertising and nonadvertising was getting blurry, as with "native advertisements" (i.e. ads that have a similar look and feel to the rest of the content) or product placements (e.g. companies paying YouTube or Instagram "influencers" to use a product). Rather, it seemed that *everything* was now becoming an ad.

The confluence of these trends has given us the digital "attention economy", the environment in which digital products and services relentlessly compete to capture and exploit our attention. In the attention economy, winning means getting as many people as possible to spend as much time and attention as possible with one's product or service. Although, as it's often said, in the attention economy "the user *is* the product."

Think about it: The attention you're deploying in order to read this book right now (an attention for which, by the way, I'm grateful) – an attention that includes, among other things, the saccades of your eyeballs, the information flows of your executive control function, your daily stockpile of willpower, and the goals you hope reading this book will help you achieve – these and other processes you use to navigate your life are *literally* the object of competition among many of the technologies you use every day. There are *literally* billions of dollars being spent to figure out how to get you to look at one thing over another; to buy one thing over another; to care about one thing over another. This is *literally* the design purpose of many of the technologies you trust to guide your life every day.

Because there's *so* much competition for our attention, designers inevitably have to appeal to the lowest parts of us – they have to privilege our impulses over our intentions even *further* – and exploit the catalog of decision-making biases that psychologists and behavioral economists have been diligently compiling over the last few decades. These biases include things like loss aversion (such as the "fear of missing out," often abbreviated as FOMO), social comparison, the status quo bias, framing effects, anchoring effects, and countless others.[16] My friend Tristan Harris has a nice phrase for this cheap exploitation of our vulnerabilities: the "race to the bottom of the brain stem."[17]

Clickbait is emblematic of this petty competition for our attention. Although the word is of recent coinage, "clickbait" has already been enshrined in the *Oxford English Dictionary*, where it's defined as "content whose main purpose is to attract attention and encourage visitors to click on a link to a particular web page." You've no doubt come across clickbait on the web, even if you haven't known it by name. It's marked by certain recognizable and rage-inducing headline patterns, as seen in, for example: "23 Things Parents Should Never Apologize For," "This One Surprising Phrase Will Make You Seem More Polite," or "This Baby Panda Showed Up At My Door. You Won't Believe What Happened Next." Clickbait laser-targets our emotions: a study of 100 million articles shared on Facebook found that the most common phrases in "top-performing" headlines were phrases such as "are freaking out," "make you cry," and "shocked to see." It also found that headlines which "appeal to a sense of tribal belonging" drive increased engagement, for instance those of the formulation "X things only [some group] will understand."[18]

In the attention economy, this is the game *all* persuasive design must play – not only the writers of headlines. In fact, there's a burgeoning industry of authors and consultants helping designers of all sorts draw on the latest research in behavioral science to punch the right buttons in our brains as effectively and reliably as possible.[19]

One major aim of such persuasive design is to keep users coming back to a product repeatedly, which requires the creation of habits. The closest thing to a bible for designers who want to induce habits in their users is probably Nir Eyal's book *Hooked: How to Build Habit Forming Products*. "Technologists build products meant to persuade people to do what we want them to do," Eyal writes. "We call these people 'users' and even if we don't say it aloud, we secretly wish every one of them would become fiendishly hooked to whatever we're making."[20] In the book, Eyal gives designers a four-stage model for hooking users that consists of a trigger, an action, a variable reward, and the user's "investment" in the product (e.g. of time or money).

The key element here is the variable reward. When you randomize the reward schedule for a given action, it increases the number of times a person is likely to take that action.[21] This is the underlying dynamic at work behind the high engagement users have with "infinite" scrolling feeds, especially those with "pull-to-refresh" functionality, which we find in countless applications and websites today such as Facebook's News Feed or Twitter's Stream. It's also used widely in all sorts of video games. In fact, this effect is often referred to as the "slot machine" effect, because it's the foundational mechanism on which the machine gambling industry relies – and which generates for them over a billion dollars in revenue every day in the United States alone.[22] Variable reward scheduling is also the engine of the compulsive, and sometimes addictive, habits of usage that many users struggle to control.[23]

Whether we're using a slot machine or an app that's designed to "hook" us, we're doing the same thing; we're "paying for the possibility of a surprise."[24] With slot machines, we pay with our money. With technologies in the attention economy, we pay with our attention. And, as with slot machines, the benefits we receive from these technologies – namely "free" products and services – are up front and immediate, whereas we pay the attentional costs in small denominations distributed over time. Rarely do we realize how costly our free things are.

Persuasive design isn't inherently *bad*, of course, even when it does appeal to our psychological biases. Indeed, it can be used for our benefit. In the area of public policy, for instance, the practice of "nudging" aims to structure people's environments in ways that help them make decisions that better promote their well-being. However, in the attention economy the incentives for persuasive design reward grabbing, and holding, our attention – keeping us looking, clicking, tapping, and scrolling. This amplifies, rather than mitigates, the challenges of self-regulation we already face in the era of information abundance.

On the opening screen of one of the first web browsers there was a notice that read, "There is no 'top' to the World Wide Web."[25] In other words, the web isn't categorized hierarchically, like a directory of files – it's decentralized, a network of nodes. One of the tragic ironies about the internet is that such a decentralized infrastructure of *information* management could enable the most centralized systems of *attention* management in human history. Today, just a few people at a handful of companies now have the ability to shape what billions of human beings think and do. One person, Mark Zuckerberg, owns Facebook, which has over 2 billion users, as well as WhatsApp (1.3 billion users), Facebook Messenger (1.2 billion users), and Instagram (800 million users).[26] Google and Facebook now comprise 85 percent (and rising) of internet advertising's year-over-year growth.[27] And the Facebook News Feed is now the primary source of traffic for news websites.[28]

Alexander the Great could never have dreamed of having this amount of power. We don't even have a good word for it yet. This isn't a currently categorizable form of control over one's fellow human beings. It's more akin to a new government or religion, or even language. But even these categories feel insufficient. There aren't even 2 billion English speakers in the world.

In 1943, in the thick of World War II, Winston Churchill traveled to Harvard to pick up an honorary degree and say a few words to a packed house. The title of his talk was "The Gift of a Common Tongue." After lauding the fact that Britain and America shared a common language – which, he hoped, might one day serve as the basis not only for Anglo-American fraternity and solidarity, but even for a common citizenship – he gave a plug to Basic English, a simplified version of English that he hoped might one day become a global lingua franca, a "medium, albeit primitive, of intercourse and understanding." This was the context – the prospect of giving the world a common linguistic operating system – in which he said "the empires of the future are the empires of the mind."

The corollary of Churchill's maxim is that the *freedoms* of the future are the *freedoms* of the mind. His future was the present we now struggle to see. Yet when the light falls on it just right, we can see the clear and urgent threat that this unprecedented system of intelligent, industrialized persuasion poses to our freedom of attention.

NOTES

1 Aesop, "The North Wind and the Sun." Perry Index 46.
2 Redström, Johan (2006). Persuasive Design: Fringes and Foundations. *Persuasive Technology*, 112–122.
3 Goss, Jon (1993). The "Magic of the Mall": An Analysis of Form, Function, and Meaning in the Contemporary Retail Built Environment. *Annals of the Association of American Geographers*, 83 (1), 18–47. https://doi.org/10.1111/j.1467-8306.1993.tb01921.x
4 Churchill, Winston (1943). House of Commons Rebuilding (pp. 403–406). www.winstonchurchill.org/resources/speeches/1941-1945-war-leader/the-price-of-greatness-is-responsibility/
5 Simonite, Tom (2016). How Google Plans to Solve Artificial Intelligence. *MIT Technology Review*. www.technologyreview.com/s/601139/how-google-plans-to-solve-artificial-intelligence/. Rowan, David (2015). DeepMind: Inside Google's Super-brain. WIRED. www.wired.co.uk/article/deepmind
6 Singel, Ryan (2010). OCT. 27, 1994: Web Gives Birth to Banner Ads. WIRED. www.wired.com/2010/10/1027hotwired-banner-ads
7 eMarketer Report (2017). Worldwide Ad Spending: The eMarketer Forecast for 2017. www.emarketer.com/Report/Worldwide-Ad-Spending-eMarketer-Forecast-2017/2002019
8 Vance, Ashlee (2011). This Tech Bubble is Different. *Bloomberg Businessweek*, April 14.
9 Samuels, J., Eaton, W. W., Bienvenu, O. J., Brown, C. H., Costa, P. T. and Nestadt, G. (2002). Prevalence and Correlates of Personality Disorders in a Community Sample. *British Journal of Psychiatry: The Journal of Mental Science*, 180 (6), 536–542. https://doi.org/10.1192/BJP.180.6.536. Tversky, Amos and Kahneman, Daniel (1973). Availability: A Heuristic for Judging Frequency and Probability. *Cognitive Psychology*, 5 (2), 207–232. https://doi.org/10.1016/0010-0285(73)90033-9
10 Bargh, John A. and Chartrand, Tanya L. (1999). The Unbearable Automaticity of Being. *American Psychologist*, 54 (7), 462.

11 Crisp, Roger (1987). Persuasive Advertising, Autonomy, and the Creation of Desire. *Journal of Business Ethics*, 6 (5), 413–418.

12 Bradt, George (2016). Wanamaker was Wrong – The Vast Majority of Advertising is Wasted. *Forbes*, September 14.

13 Turow, Joseph (2012). *The Daily You: How the New Advertising Industry is Defining your Identity and your Worth*. New Haven, CT: Yale University Press.

14 Barth, A. (2011). HTTP State Management Mechanism. Internet Engineering Task Force. https://tools.ietf.org/html/rfc6265

15 Lawson, Matt (2015). Under the Hood: How Google AdWords Measures Store Visits. Search Engine Land, June 18. https://searchengineland.com/hood-google-adwords-measures-store-visits-222905

16 Kahneman, Daniel (2012). *Thinking, Fast and Slow*. New York: Farrar, Straus and Giroux. Przybylski, A. K., Murayama, K., DeHaan, C. R. and Gladwell, V. (2013). Motivational, Emotional, and Behavioral Correlates of Fear of Missing Out. *Computers in Human Behavior*, 29 (4), 1841–1848.

17 Harris, Tristan (2016). How Technology Hijacks People's Minds – From a Magician and Google's Design Ethicist. Thrive Global, May 18. https://journal.thriveglobal.com/how-technology-hijacks-peoples-minds-from-a-magician-and-google-s-design-ethicist-56d62ef5edf3

18 Rayson, Steve (2017). We Analyzed 100 Million Headlines. Here's What We Learned. Buzzsumo, June 26. http://buzzsumo.com/blog/most-shared-headlines-study/

19 Fogg, B. J. (2003). *Persuasive Technology: Using Computers to Change What We Think and Do*. Burlington, MA: Morgan Kaufmann. Parr, Martin (2015). The Selfie Stick. www.martinparr.com/2015/the-selfie-stick/

20 Eyal, Nir (2014). *Hooked: How to build Habit-Forming Products*. London: Portfolio Penguin.

21 Ferster, C. B. and Skinner, B. F. (1957). *Schedules of Reinforcement*. East Norwalk, CT: Appleton-Century-Crofts.

22 Rivlin, Gary (2007). Slot Machines for the Young and Active. *New York Times*, December 10.

23 Schüll, Natasha (2014). *Addiction by Design: Machine Gambling in Las Vegas*. Princeton University Press.

24 Kincaid, Harold and Ross, Don (eds.) (2009). *The Oxford Handbook of Philosophy of Economics*. Oxford University Press.

25 Electronic Frontier Foundation (1994). https://w2.eff.org/Net_culture/
    Net_info/EFF_Net_Guide/EEGTTI_HTML/eeg_213.html
26 Statista (2017). www.statista.com/markets/424/topic/540/social-media-
    user-generated-content/
27 FastCompany (2017). Google and Facebook Now Own 85% of Internet
    Ad Growth. www.fastcompany.com/4039263/google-and-facebook-now-
    own-85-of-internet-ad-growth
28 Lee, Timothy B. (2016). Mark Zuckerberg is in Denial About How
    Facebook is Harming our Politics. Vox, November 10. www.vox.com/new-
    money/2016/11/6/13509854/facebook-politics-news-bad

11 Clicks against Humanity

6 The Citizen is the Product

I keep a list of things that have no name but need one. Like the feeling you get when you stare at a word so long that it looks like it's spelled wrong. Or that social glitch that happens when you're about to pass someone on the sidewalk, but neither of you can tell which side the other wants to walk on, so when the moment comes you both do that jerky little stutter-step thing that somehow, miraculously, always manages to resolve itself. Or when you're sitting in a chair and someone walks behind you, and you scoot forward to give them room to pass even when you don't need to, just to acknowledge their existence and the fact that they're passing. Or when you're in a taxi and your driver maneuvers in some way that cuts off another driver or pedestrian, and your impulse is to apologize to them because it's your taxi and you benefitted from his transgression, but on the other hand it wasn't *your* fault, so as you pass the aggrieved party you make some token gesture out the window, like a little pinched-lip half-smile, as though to half-assedly signal "Sorry!"

"The limits of my language," wrote the philosopher Ludwig Wittgenstein, "mean the limits of my world."[1] We expand our awareness, both of ourselves and of our world, when we expand our language. We see things we didn't know to see before, and we learn how to talk about them with others.[2] What *did* we call "clickbait" before that word came into being? Or "binge-watching," or "humblebrag," or "FOMO"?

Diogenes also needed to coin new terms to describe the way he wanted to relate to the world. When people asked him where he was from, he replied that he was "a citizen of the world" – a *kosmopolitês*, or "cosmopolitan."[3] No one had ever said this before, so no one knew what it meant. The term certainly didn't have the connotation it has today: Diogenes was no moneyed jet-setter. In fact, at one point in his life Diogenes was put on sale as a slave. It's said that when the slave-master brought him before a group of potential buyers, he directed Diogenes to tell them what he could do. Diogenes retorted, "Govern men." One potential buyer was so impressed by this reply that he immediately purchased Diogenes and put him in charge of educating his children. The "citizen of the world," it seemed, had become the product.

We need new words to describe how we want to relate to our new empires of the mind. A vast project of industrialized persuasion has emerged under our feet. It competes to capture and exploit our attention, and we want to account for the ways this threatens the success of our personal and political lives. What we need, then, is a richer and more capacious way of talking about attention. As Tony Judt writes in *Ill Fares the Land*, "you must be able to name a problem if you wish to solve it."[4]

However, in our societal and political discussions we lack such a language. As a result, we've failed to account for the wider set of technological "distractions" that threaten us most. We still grapple with attention using conceptual tools developed in environments of information scarcity. We don't have a way of thinking about attention as a *thing*. The limits of our language are the limits of our attentional world.

What *is* attention? "Everyone knows what attention is," wrote William James in his 1899 text *The Principles of Psychology*. In reality, no one *really* knows what attention is. (And I'm not just taking the contrary position because my name happens to be the inverse of his.) The term "attention" is used in many different ways across a wide range of domains.[5] In fact, even within the narrowly specialized psychology and neuroscience literatures, researchers can't seem to agree.[6]

Generally speaking, though, when we use the term "attention" in day-to-day parlance, we typically mean what cognitive scientists call the "spotlight" of attention, or the direction of our moment-to-moment awareness within the immediate task domain.[7] The "spotlight" of attention is the sort of attention that helps us do what we want to do. It includes the way I'm selecting certain pieces of information from my sensory stream as I write this: I'm looking at a certain section of my computer screen; I'm typing a particular key on my keyboard. (In fact, just as I was writing the previous sentence, a helicopter went *whopwhopwhop* past my window and disappeared behind a tree, momentarily distracting the spotlight of my attention.)

Yet this is exactly the surface-level sort of "distraction" at which our day-to-day language about attention already operates. Expanding our language means diving down to deeper levels of attention. How can we access those deeper levels with a view to clarifying the distinct challenges of the attention economy?

Perhaps pivoting our question may help. Rather than asking "What is attention?", I wonder whether a better question would be, "What do we pay when we 'pay' attention?" In this light, new spaces of possibility open up that allow us to venture well beyond the domain of the "spotlight" of attention.

What *do* you pay when you pay attention? You pay with all the things you could have attended to, but didn't: all the goals you didn't pursue, all the actions you didn't take, and all the possible yous you could have been, had you attended to those other things. Attention is paid in possible futures forgone. You pay for that extra *Game of Thrones* episode with the heart-to-heart talk you could have had with your anxious child. You pay for that extra hour on social media with the sleep you didn't get and the fresh feeling you didn't have the next morning. You pay for giving in to that outrage-inducing piece of clickbait about that politician you hate with the patience and empathy it took from you, and the anger you have at yourself for allowing yourself to take the bait in the first place.

We pay attention with the lives we might have lived. When we consider the opportunity costs in this wider view, the question of attention extends far beyond the next turn in your life's GPS: it encompasses *all* the turns and their relations, the nature of your destination, the specific *way* you want to get there, *why* you're going there, and also your ability to ask any of these questions in the first place. In this view, the question of attention becomes the question of having the freedom to navigate your life in the way you want, across all scales of the human experience.

The great thinkers on the question of freedom can be of use here, in particular the nineteenth-century British philosopher John Stuart Mill. In his seminal text *On Liberty*, Mill writes that the "appropriate region of human liberty ... comprises, first, the inward domain of consciousness ... liberty of thought and feeling; absolute freedom of opinion and sentiment on all subjects, practical or specu-lative." "This principle," he writes, "requires liberty of tastes and pursuits; of framing the plan of our life to suit our own character."[8] Here, Mill seems to me to be articulating something *like* a freedom of attention. Crucially, he points out that freedom of the mind is the *first* freedom, upon which freedom of expression depends. The freedom of speech is meaningless without the freedom of attention, which is both its complement and its prerequisite.

But Mill also gives us a clue here about how we might think more broadly about attention – how we might take into account the full range of potential harms to which our "almost infinite appetite for distractions" might fall prey. So attention isn't just about what you're doing right now. It's about the way you navigate your whole life: it's about who you are, who you want to be, and the way you define and pursue those things.

This suggests that we need to move beyond a narrowly psych-ologized notion of attention. Georg Franck writes, "Attention is far more than just the ready supply of information processing capacity. Attention is the essence of being conscious in the sense of both self-certain existence and alert presence of mind. Attention is the medium in which everything must be represented that is to become real for us as experiencing creatures."[9] This is an intriguing direction in which to take the concept of attention. However, for our present purposes it seems overly broad.

Perhaps William James's description of "effort of attention" as "the essential phenomenon of will" points the way to a narrower and more useful middle ground. If we expand our notion of "attention" in the direction of conceptions of the human will, this may allow us to take a view that's wide enough to include more than just the immediate "spotlight," but not so ultra-wide that it encompasses totalizing concepts such as "consciousness," "being," "life itself," and so on. I'm not arguing here that we should think of attention as *coextensive* with the human will, but rather as a construct that we can usefully expand in that general direction. For our present purposes, we might think of this widened view of "attention" as the full stack of navigational capacities across all levels of human life.

The will is, of course, also the source of the authority of democracy. In this light, the political and moral implications of the digital attention economy start to move into the foreground. Article 21 of the Universal Declaration of Human Rights states, "The will of the people shall be the basis of the authority of government." If the digital attention economy were compromising the human will, it would therefore be striking at the very foundations of democracy. This would directly threaten not only individual freedom and autonomy, but also our collective ability to pursue any politics worth having.

Of course, the "luminous conception" of the general will Rousseau writes about is not merely the aggregation of individual wills: it's the joined will of individuals where they are all "concerned with the common interest." That is to say, an individual can have a personal will that is contrary or dissimilar to the general will that he has as a citizen. So the political implications of undermining attention, in this broader sense, are not fully accounted for by considering merely the frustrated navigation of an individual's life, or even the frustrated navigation of many individuals' lives. We must also account for the unique frustrations of the citizen, and possibly even the very idea of citizenship itself. Rousseau writes that if society were understood as a "body," then "there would be a kind of common sensorium which would ensure that all parts are coordinated." Following this metaphor, undermining the very construct of citizenship would be akin to short-circuiting the nervous system that coordinates the body politic. Indeed, there are many types of group decision-making biases and fallacies that psychology research has identified which routinely lead to collective action that does not reflect the collective will (and sometimes, as in the "Abilene Paradox," even reflects its opposite).[10]

Can we expand the language of attention and use it to talk across questions of both individual and general will in order to clarify the threats the intelligent, industrialized persuasion of the attention economy poses to life and politics?

If we accept this broader view of attention as something akin to the operation of the human will, and we pair it with an understanding of the centrality of the human will for politics, then it's hard to avoid viewing the attention economy as a project that ultimately targets and shapes the foundations of our politics. It is not merely the user, but indeed the citizen, who is the product.

To develop this wider notion of "attention" in the direction of the will, both individual and collective, let's assume (at least for now) two more types of attention – two more "lights" – in addition to the "spotlight" of immediate awareness. These "lights" broadly align with the way the philosopher Harry Frankfurt views the structure of the human will.

It's important to note here that I'm not making any sort of scientific claim or argument with these distinctions. My interest is primarily exploratory: think of this as one possible heuristic that may be useful for piercing through this problem space. Gordon Pask once called cybernetics "the art and science of manipulating defensible metaphors."[11] This is a fitting description for our task here as well.

The "Spotlight"   Our immediate capacities for navigating awareness and action toward tasks. Enables us to do what we want to do.

The "Starlight"   Our broader capacities for navigating life "by the stars" of our higher goals and values. Enables us to be who we want to be.

The "Daylight"   Our fundamental capacities – such as reflection, metacognition, reason, and intelligence – that enable us to define our goals and values to begin with. Enables us to "want what we want to want."

These three "lights" of attention pertain to *doing*, *being*, and *knowing*, respectively. When each of these "lights" gets obscured, a distinct – though not mutually exclusive – type of "distraction" results.

NOTES

1 Wittgenstein, Ludwig (1921). *Tractatus Logico-Philosophicus*, trans. C. K. Ogden. New York: Dover, 1999.

2 Kay, Paul and Kempton, Willett (1984). What is the Sapir-Whorf Hypothesis? *American Anthropological Society*, March.

3 Diogenes Laertius vi. 63; Arrian VII.2.

4 Judt, Tony (2011). *Ill Fares the Land: A Treatise on our Present Discontents*. Harmondsworth: Penguin.

5 Rogers, Kenneth (2014). *The Attention Complex*. New York, NY: Palgrave Macmillan.

6 Nobre, Anna C. and Kastner, Sabine (eds.) (2014). *The Oxford Handbook of Attention*. Oxford University Press.

7 Lavie, Nilli (2005). Distracted and Confused?: Selective Attention Under Load. *Trends in Cognitive Sciences*, 9 (2), 75–82.

8 Mill, John Stuart (1859). *On Liberty*. London: Longman, Roberts & Green.

9 Franck, Georg (1999). The Economy of Attention. *Merkur*, 534/535.

10 Harvey, Jerry B. (1988). *The Abilene Paradox and Other Meditations on Management*. San Francisco, CA: Jossey-Bass.

11 Pask, Gordon (1975). *The Cybernetics of Human Learning and Performance*. London: Hutchinson

7   The Spotlight

At Netflix, we are competing for our customers' time, so our competitors include Snapchat, YouTube, sleep, etc.

Reed Hastings, CEO, Netflix

Bob Dylan said, "A man is a success if he gets up in the morning and gets to bed at night, and in between he does what he wants to do."[1] Sometimes our technologies help us do what we want to do. Other times they don't. When our technologies fail us in this regard, they undermine the "spotlight" of our attention. This produces *functional* distractions that direct us away from information or actions relevant to our immediate tasks or goals.

Functional distraction is what's commonly meant by the word "distraction" in day-to-day use. This is the sort of distraction that Huxley called the "mere casual waste products of psychophysiological activity."[2] Like when you sit down at a computer to fulfill all the plans you've made, to do all those very responsible and adult things you know at the back of your mind you absolutely *must* do, and yet you don't: instead, your unconscious mind outruns your conscious mind, and you find yourself, forty-five minutes later, having read articles about the global economic meltdown, having watched autoplaying YouTube videos about dogs who were running while sleeping, and having voyeured the life achievements of some astonishing percentage of people who are willing to publicly admit that they know you, however little it may actually be the case.

Functional distractions commonly come from notifications. Each day, the Android mobile operating system alone sends over *11 billion* notifications to its more than 1 billion users. We widely encounter notifications from systems such as email services, social networks, and mobile applications. For instance, "I was going to turn on the kettle so I could make some tea, but then Candy Crush reminded me I haven't played in a few days." Another major source of notifications is person-to-person communication, as in instant messaging applications. Often, as in Google's Gmail system, notifications are colored red and placed in the upper-right corner of the user's vision in order to better grab their attention and maximize the persuasive effect. This effect relies on the human reaction to the color red,[3] as well as the cleaning/grooming instinct,[4] which often makes it hard to resist clicking on the notifications.

The effects of interruptions aren't limited to the amount of time we lose engaging with them directly. When a person is in a focus state and gets interrupted, it takes on average twenty-three minutes for them to regain their focus. In addition, experiencing a functional distraction in your environment can make it harder to return your attention to that same place in your environment later if something task-salient appears there.[5] Also, functional distractions may direct your attention away not merely from perceptual information, but also from reflective information. For example, when an app notification or instant message from another person interrupts your focus or "flow," it may introduce information that crowds out other task-relevant information in your working memory.[6] In other words, the persuasive designs of the attention economy compete not only against one another for your attention, but also against things in your inner environment as well. Furthermore, exposure to repeated notifications can create mental habits that train users to interrupt themselves, even in the absence of the technologies themselves.[7] We tend to overlook the harms of functional distraction due to the bite-size nature of its influence. However, as the philosopher Matthew Crawford writes, "Distractibility might be regarded as the mental equivalent of obesity." From this perspective, individual functional distractions can be viewed as akin to individual potato chips.

Undermining the spotlight of attention can frustrate our political lives in several ways. One is by distracting us away from political information and toward some nonpolitical type of information. This effect doesn't necessarily have to be consciously engineered. For instance, a news website might give me the option of viewing the latest update on my government's effort to reform tax policy, but it may place it on the page next to another article with a headline that's teasing some juicy piece of celebrity gossip – and whose photo is undoubtedly better at speaking to my automatic self and getting me to click.

At the same time, distraction away from political information *could* occur by design, for instance via the propagandizing efforts of a political party or some other interested actor. For example, the Chinese government has been known to censor information online that they deem objectionable by suppressing or removing it. However, their propaganda organization, commonly known as the "50 Cent Party," has recently begun using a technique called "reverse censorship," or "strategic distraction," to drown out the offending information with a torrent of other social media content that directs people's attention away from the objectionable material. The Harvard researchers who carried out a study analyzing these efforts estimate that the Chinese government creates 448 million posts on social media per year as part of this strategic distraction.[8] As researcher Margaret Roberts said in an interview, "the point isn't to get people to believe or care about the propaganda; it's to get them to pay less attention to stories the government wants to suppress."[9]

A "strategic distraction" may also be used to change the focus of a political debate. Here it is hard to avoid discussion of US President Donald J. Trump's use of the Twitter microblogging platform. A major function of his Twitter use has been to deflect attention away from scandalous or embarrassing news stories that may reflect poorly on him. Similarly, in the 2016 US presidential election, he used his so-called "tweetstorms" to "take all of the air out of the room," in other words, to gain the attention of television and radio news broadcasters and thereby capture as much of their finite airtime as possible, leaving little airtime for other candidates to capture. One study estimated that eight months before the 2016 election, he had already captured almost \$2 billion worth of free or "earned" media coverage.[10] In addition to this bulk approach, he also deployed highly targeted functional distraction. For example, consider his campaign's voter suppression efforts, which used Facebook to send highly targeted messages to African Americans (techniques which, while outrageous, used fairly standard digital advertising methods).[11]

Functional distraction can certainly be politically consequential, but it's unlikely that an isolated instance of a compromised "spotlight" would pose the sort of fundamental risk to individual and collective will that we're ultimately concerned with addressing here. To identify those deeper risks, it's necessary to move quickly to the deeper types of distraction.

NOTES

1 Dylan, Bob (2006). *Dylan, The Essential Interviews*, ed. J. Cott. New York, NY: Wenner Books.

2 Huxley, Aldous and Smith, Huston (2013). Distractions-I. *The Divine Within: Selected Writings on Enlightenment*. New York, NY: Harper Perennial.

3 Elliot, A. J., Maier, M. A., Moller, A. C., Friedman, R. and Meinhardt, J. (2007). Color and Psychological Functioning: The Effect of Red on Performance Attainment. *Journal of Experimental Psychology*, 136 (1), 154–168.

4 Curtis, Valerie A. (2007). Dirt, Disgust and Disease: A Natural History of Hygiene. *Journal of Epidemiology and Community Health*, 61, 660–664.

5 Posner, M. I., Rafal, R. D., Choate, L. S. and Vaughan, J. (1985). Inhibition of Return: Neural Basis and Function. *Cognitive Neuropsychology*, 2 (3), 211–228.

6 Csikszentmihalyi, Mihaly (2008). *Flow: The Psychology of Optimal Experience*. New York, NY: Harper Perennial.

7 Mark, G., Gudith, D. and Klocke, U. (2008). The Cost of Interrupted Work: More Speed and Stress. Proceedings of the SIGCHI Conference on Human Factors in Computing Systems.

8 King, G., Pan, J., Roberts, M. E., Allen, D., Bol, P., Fair, B. and Zheng, C. (2017). How the Chinese Government Fabricates Social Media Posts for Strategic Distraction, Not Engaged Argument. Research article. https:// gking.harvard.edu/files/gking/files/50c.pdf

9 Illing, Sean (2017). China is Perfecting a New Method for Suppressing Dissent on the Internet. Vox, August 2. www.vox.com/world/2017/8/2/ 16019562/china-russia-internet-propaganda-media

10 Confessore, Nicholas and Yourish, Karen (2016). $2 Billion Worth of Free Media for Donald Trump. *New York Times*, March 16. www.nytimes.com/ 2016/03/16/upshot/measuring-donald-trumps-mammoth-advantage-in-free-media.html

11 Green, Joshua and Issenberg, Sasha (2016). Inside the Trump Bunker, with 12 Days to Go. *Bloomberg Businessweek*, October 27. www.bloomberg.com/ news/articles/2016-10-27/inside-the-trump-bunker-with-12-days-to-go

8 The Starlight

[Donald Trump's candidacy] may not be good for America, but it's damn good for CBS.

Les Moonves (CBS Chairman/CEO), February 2016

Around the time I started feeling existentially compromised by the deep distractions collecting in my life, I developed a habit that quickly became annoying to everyone around me. It went like this: I'd hear someone use a phrase to describe me that had a certain ring to it, like it would make a good title for something – but its content was both specific and odd enough that if it *were* used as the title for a biography about my whole life, it would be utterly absurd. Whenever I'd hear a phrase like that, I'd repeat it with the gravitas of a movie-trailer announcer, and then follow it with the phrase: "The James Williams Story."

Here's an example. One day, after a long conversation with my wife, she said to me, "You're, like, my receptacle of secrets." To which I replied: *"Receptacle of Secrets: The James Williams Story."* The joke being, of course, that choosing this one random, specific snapshot of my life to represent the narrative of my entire existence – an existence which has involved many achievements more notable than hearing and keeping the odd spousal secret – would be an absurd and arbitrary thing to do. I eventually came to understand (or perhaps rationalize) this habit as a playful, shorthand way of stabilizing what philosophers would call my "diachronic self," or the self over time, over the increasingly rocky waves of my "synchronic self," or the self at a given moment. I might have been overanalyzing it, but I interpreted this emergent habit as a way of pushing back against my immediate environment's ability to define me. It was a way of saying, "I will not be so easily summarized!"

It was a way of trying to hold onto my story by calling attention to what my story definitely was *not*.

We experience our identities as stories, according to a line of thought known as "narrative identity theory."[1] In his book *Neuroethics*, Neil Levy writes that both synchronic and diachronic unity are essential for helping us maintain the integrity of these stories: "We want to live a life that expresses our central values, and we want that life to make *narrative* sense: we want to be able to tell ourselves and others a story, which explains where we come from, how we got to where we are, and where we are going" (p. 201).

When we lose the story of our identities, whether on individual or collective levels, it undermines what we could call the "starlight" of our attention, or our ability to navigate "by the stars" of our higher values or "being goals." When our "starlight" is obscured, it makes it harder to "be who we want to be." We feel the self fragmenting and dividing, resulting in an *existential* sort of distraction. William James wrote that "our self-feeling in this world depends entirely on what we back ourselves to be and do." When we become aware that our actual habits are in dissonance with our desired values, this self-feeling often feels like a challenge to, if not the loss of, our identities.

This obscured "starlight" was a deeper layer of the distractions I'd been feeling, and I felt that the attention-grabby techniques of technology design were playing a nontrivial role. I began to realize that my technologies were enabling habits in my life that led my actions over time to diverge from the identity and values by which I wanted to live. It wasn't just that my life's GPS was guiding me into the occasional wrong turn, but rather that it had programmed me a new destination in a far-off place that it did not behoove me to visit. It was a place that valued short-term over long-term rewards, simple over complex pleasures. It felt like I was back in my high-school calculus class, and all these new technologies were souped-up versions of *Tetris*. It wasn't just that my tasks and goals were giving way to theirs – my *values* were as well.

One way I saw the "starlight" getting obscured in myself and others, in both the personal and political domains, was in the proliferation of *pettiness*. Pettiness means pursuing a low-level goal as though it were a higher, intrinsically valuable one. Low-level goals tend to be short-term goals; where this is so, pettiness may be viewed as a kind of imprudence. In *The Theory of Moral Sentiments*, Adam Smith calls prudence the virtue that's "most useful to the individual." For Smith, prudence involves the union of two things: (1) our capacity for "discerning the remote consequences of all our actions," and (2) "self-command, by which we are enabled to abstain from present pleasure or to endure present pain, in order to obtain a greater pleasure or to avoid a greater pain in some future time."

In my own life I saw this pettiness, this imprudence, manifesting in the way the social comparison dynamics of social media platforms had trained me to prioritize mere "likes" or "favorites," or to get as many "friends" or "connections" as possible, over pursuing other more meaningful relational aims. These dynamics had made me more competitive for other people's attention and affirmation than I ever remember being: I found myself spending more and more time trying to come up with clever things to say in my social posts, not because I felt they were things worth saying but because I had come to value these attentional signals for their own sake. Social interaction had become a numbers game for me, and I was focused on "winning" – even though I had no idea what winning looked like. I just knew that the more of these rewarding little social validations I got, the more of them I wanted. I was hooked.

The creators of these mechanisms didn't necessarily intend to make me, or us, into petty people. The creator of the Facebook "like" button, for instance, initially intended for it to send "little bits of positivity" to people.[2] If its design had been steered in the right way, perhaps it might have done so. However, soon enough the "like" function began to serve the data-collection and engagement-maximizing interests of advertisers. As a result, the metrics that comprised the "score" of my social game – and I, as the player of that game – were directly serving the interests of the attention economy. In the pettiness of my day-to-day number-chasing, I had lost the higher view of who I really was, or why I wanted to communicate with all these people in the first place.

Pettiness is not exactly a rare phenomenon in the political domain. However, during the 2016 US presidential election I encountered a highly moralized variant of pettiness coming from people I would have never expected to see it in. Over the course of just a few months, I witnessed several acquaintances back in Texas – good, loving people, and deeply religious "values voters" – go from vocally rejecting one particular candidate as being morally reprehensible and utterly unacceptable, to ultimately setting aside those foundational moral commitments in the name of securing a short-term political win. By the time a video emerged of the candidate bragging about committing sexual assault, this petty overwriting of moral commitment with political expediency was so total as to render this staggering development barely shrug-worthy. By then, their posts on social media were saying things like, "I care more about what Hillary *did* than what Trump *said!*"

In the 2016 presidential election campaign, Donald Trump took the dominance of pettiness over prudence to new heights. Trump is very straightforwardly an embodiment of the dynamics of clickbait: he's the logical product (though not endpoint) in the political domain of a petty media environment defined by impulsivity and zero-sum competition for our attention. One analyst has estimated that Trump is worth $2 billion to Twitter, which amounts to almost one-fifth of the company's current value.[3] His success metrics – number of rally attendees, number of retweets – are attention economy metrics. Given this, it's remarkable how consistently societal discussion has completely misread him by casting him in *informational*, rather than *attentional*, terms. Like clickbait or so-called "fake news," the design goal of Trump is not to inform but to induce. Content is incidental to effect.

At its extreme, this pettiness can manifest as narcissism, a preoccupation with being recognized by others, valuing attention for its own sake, and the prioritization of fame as a core value. A meta-analysis of fifty-seven studies found that social media in particular is linked with increased narcissism.[4] Another study found that young people are now getting more plastic surgery due to pressure from social media.[5] And a study of children's television shows in recent years found that, rather than pro-social community values, the main value now held up by children's television shows as being most worth pursuing is *fame*.[6] In his historical study of fame *The Frenzy of Renown*, Leo Braudy writes that when we call someone "famous," what we're fundamentally saying is, "pay attention to this." So it's entirely to be expected that in an age of information abundance and attention scarcity we would see an increased reliance on fame as a heuristic for determining what and who matters (i.e. merits our attention), as well as an increased desire for achieving fame in one's own lifetime (as opposed to a legacy across generations).[7]

Sometimes the desire for fame can have life-and-death consequences. Countless YouTube personalities walk on the edges of skyscrapers, chug whole bottles of liquor, and perform other dangerous stunts, all for the fame – and the advertising revenue – it might bring them. The results are sometimes tragic. In June 2017 a man concocted an attention-getting YouTube stunt in which he instructed his wife, who was then pregnant with their second child, to shoot a handgun from point-blank range at a thick book he was holding in front of his chest. The bullet ripped through the book and struck and killed him. As the *New York Times* reported:

> It was a preventable death, the sheriff said, apparently fostered by a culture in which money and some degree of stardom can be obtained by those who attract a loyal internet following with their antics.

In the couple's last video, posted on Monday, Ms. Perez and her boyfriend considered what it would be like to be one of those stars – "when we have 300,000 subscribers."

"The bigger we get, I'll be throwing parties," Mr. Ruiz said. "Why not?"[8]

Similarly, on the video-game live-streaming site Twitch, a 35-year-old man stayed awake to continue his streaming marathon for so long that he died.[9] And in December 2017, Wu Yongning, a Chinese man known as a "rooftopper" – someone who dangles from skyscrapers without safety equipment in order to post and monetize the video online – fell to his death. As one user on the Chinese microblogging service Weibo reflected about the role, and responsibility, of the man's approving audience members:

Watching him and praising him was akin to ... buying a knife for someone who wanted to stab himself, or encouraging someone who wants to jump off a building. ... Don't click "like," don't click "follow." This is the least we can do to try to save someone's life.[10]

There's nothing wrong with wanting attention from other people. Indeed, it's only human. Receiving the attention of others is a necessary, and often quite meaningful, part of human life. In fact, Adam Smith argues in *Wealth of Nations* that it's the main reason we pursue wealth in the first place: "To be attended to, to be taken notice of with sympathy, complacency, and approbation," he writes, "are all the advantages which we can propose to derive from it." It's this approval, this regard from others, he says, that leads people to pursue wealth – and when they *do* attain wealth, and then "expend it," it's *that* expenditure – what we might call the exchange of monetary wealth for attentional, or reputational, wealth – that Smith describes as being "led by an invisible hand."[11] So, on a certain reading, one could argue that *all* economies are ultimately economies of attention. However, this doesn't mean that all attention is worth receiving, or that all ways of pursuing it are praiseworthy.

We can also see the obscuring of our starlight in the erosion of our sense of the nature and importance of our higher values. In Mike Judge's film *Idiocracy*, a man awakes from cryogenic slumber in a distant future where everyone has become markedly stupider. At one point in the story he visits a shambolic Costco warehouse store, where a glazed-eyed front-door greeter welcomes him by mechanically droning, "Welcome to Costco. I love you." This is an extreme example of the dilution of a higher value – in this case, love. In the design of digital technologies, persuasive goals often go by names that sound lofty and virtuous but have been similarly diluted: "relevance," "engagement," "smart," and so on. Designing users' lives toward diluted values leads to the dilution of their *own* values at both individual and collective levels.

Consider that across many liberal democracies the percentage of people who say it's "essential" to live in a democracy has in recent years been in freefall. The "starlight" of democratic values seems to be dimming across diverse cultures, languages, and economic situations. However, one of the few factors these countries *do* have in common is their dominant form of media, which just happens to be the largest, most standardized, and most centralized form of attentional control in human history, and which also happens to distract from our "starlight" by design.

Similarly, in the last two decades the percentage of Americans who approve of military rule (saying it would be either "good" or "very good") has doubled, according to the World Values Survey, to now being one in six people.[12] The authors of a noted study on this topic point out that this percentage "has risen in most mature democracies, including Germany, Sweden, and the United Kingdom." Crucially, they also note that this trend can't be attributed to economic hardship. "Strikingly," the authors write, "such undemocratic sentiments have risen especially quickly among the wealthy," and even more so among the *young* and wealthy. Today, this approval of military rule "is held by 35 percent of rich young Americans."[13]

On the part of political representatives, this value dilution manifests as the prioritization of metrics that look very much like attention economy metrics, as well as the placing of party over country. As Rousseau wrote in *Political Economy*, when a sense of duty is no longer present among political leaders, they simply focus on "fascinating the gaze of those whom they need" in order to stay in power.

Our information and communication technologies serve as mirrors for our identities, and these mirrors can show us either dignified or undignified reflections of ourselves. When we see a life in the mirror that appears to be diverging from the "stars" of freedom and self-authorship by which we want to live, our reaction not only involves the shock of indignity, but also quite often a defensive posture of "reactance." Reactance refers to the idea "that individuals have certain freedoms with regard to their behavior. If these behavioral freedoms are reduced or threatened with reduction, the individual will be motivationally aroused to regain them."[14] In other words, when we feel our freedom being restricted, we tend to want to fight to get it back.

To take one example of an undignified reflection that prompts this sort of reactance, consider the Facebook "emotional contagion" experiment that Facebook and researchers at Cornell University carried out in 2014. The experiment used the Facebook news feed to identify evidence of social contagion effects (i.e. transference of emotional valence). Over a one-week period, the experiment reduced the number of either positive or negative posts that a sample of around 700,000 Facebook users saw in their News Feed. They found that when users saw fewer negative posts, their own posts had a lower percentage of words that were negative. The same was true for positive posts and positive words. While the effect sizes were very small, the results showed a clear persuasive effect on the emotional content of users' posts.[15]

In response, some raised questions about research ethics processes – but many objections were also about the mere fact that

Facebook had manipulated its users *at all*. Clay Johnson, the founder of political marketing firm Blue State Digital, wrote, "the Facebook 'transmission of anger' experiment is terrifying."[16] The *Atlantic* described the study as "Facebook's Secret Mood Manipulation Experiment."[17] A member of the UK parliament called for an "investigation into how Facebook and other social networks manipulated emotional and psychological responses of users by editing information supplied to them."[18] And privacy activist Lauren Weinstein wrote on Twitter, "I wonder if Facebook KILLED anyone with their emotion manipulation stunt. At their scale and with depressed people out there, it's possible."[19]

We are manipulated by the design of our media all the time. This seems to me simply another way of describing what media is and does. Much, if not most, of the advertising research that occurs behind the closed doors of companies could be described as "secret mood manipulation experiments." And the investigation the UK parliamentarian called for would effectively mean investigating the design of all digital media that shape our attention in any way whatsoever.

What was unfortunately missed in the outrage cascades about this experiment was the fact that Facebook was *finally* measuring whether a given design had a positive or negative effect on people's emotions – something that they don't appear to have been doing before this time. This is precisely the sort of knowledge that allows the public to say, "We know you can measure this now – so start using it for our benefit!" But that potential response was, as it is so often, ultimately scuppered by the dynamics of the attention economy itself.

If a person were to interpret Facebook's alteration of their news feed as unacceptable manipulation, and object to the image – the "undignified reflection" – of themselves as someone who is not fully in control of their decisions about what they write in their own posts, then they would see their use of Facebook as incompatible with, and unsupportive of, the ultimate "being goal" they have for themselves. The sense of a precipitous sliding backward from that ultimate goal would, as discussed above, have the effect of undermining that person's sense of self-integrity, and would thus reduce their sense of dignity.

Finally, when we start to lose the story of our *shared* identity, it has major implications for politics. We find it harder to keep in view the commonalities we have with others in our own society. We struggle to imagine them inhabiting the same space or *demos* as us, especially when we're increasingly physically isolated from them. Division itself is not bad, of course: isolation is necessary for the development of individual views and opinions. Diversity requires division, of a sort. But the sort of division that removes the space in which the common interest and general will may be found is the sort that is extremely problematic.

This erosion of shared identity is often mischaracterized as political "polarization." However, "polarization" suggests a *rational* disunity, mere disagreement about political positions or assumptions. In essence, a disunity of *ideas*. What we have before us, on the other hand, seems a profoundly *irrational* disunity – a disunity of *identity* – and indeed a "deep-self discordance" among the body politic. This can lead to collective *akrasia*, or weakness of will. As the philosopher Charles Taylor writes, "the danger is not actual despotic control but fragmentation – that is, a people increasingly less capable of forming a common purpose and carrying it out."[20] William James, in *The Principles of Psychology*, writes, "There is no more miserable human being than one in whom nothing is habitual but indecision."[21] Perhaps we could say the same of societies as well.

Rousseau argued that a collective decision can depart from the general will if people are "misled by particular interests ... by the influence and persuasiveness of a few clever men."[22] This can, of course, happen via mere functional distraction, or inhibition of the "spotlight," but Rousseau notes that this control more often happens by subdividing society into groups, which leads them to "abandon" their "membership" of the wider group. At extremes, groups may diverge so much from one another that their insularity becomes self-reinforcing. And when this division of identity becomes moralized in such a way that it leads to a deeper sort of tribalistic delegitimizing, it veers toward a certain kind of populism, which I will discuss in the next chapter.

Here at the level of the "starlight," however, this division has primarily prompted lamentations about the problems of internet "echo chambers,"[23] or self-reinforcing "bubbles of homophily."[24] Yet the echoic metaphor seems to me to miss something essential: while echoes do bounce back, the sound ultimately dissipates. A better metaphor might be amplifier feedback, that is, holding a live microphone up to a speaker to create an instant shrieking loop that will destroy your eardrums if you let it. When the content of that shrieking loop consists of our own identities, whether individually or as groups, the distorted reflection we see in the "mirror" of technology takes on the character of a funhouse mirror, giving us only an absurd parody of ourselves.

Considering the ways my "starlight" was being obscured helped me broaden the scope of "distraction" to include not just frustrations of doing, but also frustrations of *being* over time. This sort of distraction makes us start to lose the story, at both individual and collective levels. When that happens, we start to grasp for things that feel real, true, or authentic in order to get the story back. We try to reorient our living toward the values and higher goals we want to pursue.

But here, at least, we still *know* when we're not living by our chosen stars – we can still in principle detect the errors and correct them. It seemed like there was one deeper level of "distraction" to contend with: the sort of distraction that would threaten our ability to know and define what our goals and values are in the first place.

NOTES

1 Schechtman, Marya (1996). *The Constitution of Selves*. Ithaca, NY: Cornell University Press.

2 Lewis, Paul (2017). Our Minds can be Hijacked: The Tech Insiders Who Fear a Smartphone Dystopia. *Guardian*, October 5. www.theguardian.com/technology/2017/oct/05/smartphone-addiction-silicon-valley-dystopia

3 Wittenstein, Jeran (2017). What is Trump Worth to Twitter? One Analyst Estimates $2 Billion. *Bloomberg Businessweek*, August 17. www.bloomberg.com/news/articles/2017-08-17/what-is-trump-worth-to-twitter-one-analyst-estimates-2-billion

4 Gnambs, Timo and Appel, Markus (2017). Narcissism and Social Networking Behavior: A Meta-Analysis. *Journal of Personality*, 23 March. DOI: 10.1111/jopy.12305

5 Hughes, Dominic (2017). Social Media Pressure is Linked to Cosmetic Procedure Boom. BBC News. www.bbc.com/news/health-40358138

6 Ulhs, Yalda T. and Greenfield, Patricia M. (2007). The Rise of Fame: A Historical Content Analysis. *Cyberpsychology: Journal of Psychosocial Research on Cyberspace*, 5 (1).

7 Braudy, Leo (1997). *The Frenzy of Renown: Fame and its History*. New York: Vintage.

8 Stevens, Matt (2017). A Stunt Turns Deadly for a Couple Seeking YouTube Fame. *New York Times*, August 29. www.nytimes.com/2017/06/29/us/shooting-youtube-stunt-minnesota.html

9 Devlin, K. (2017). The Mysterious Death of a Live-Streaming Gamer. BBC News. www.bbc.co.uk/news/blogs-trending-39232620

10 Wong, Tessa (2017). Wu Yongning: Who is to Blame for a Daredevil's Death? BBC News. www.bbc.com/news/world-asia-china-42335014

11 Smith, Adam (1776). *The Wealth of Nations*.

12 Taub, Amanda (2016). How Stable are Democracies? Warning Signs are Flashing Red. *New York Times*, November 29. www.nytimes.com/2016/11/29/world/americas/western-liberal-democracy.html

13 Foa, R. S., Mounk, Y., Inglehart, R. F., Carter, B. L., Yarwood, J., Reyntjens, F., Watanabe, A. (2016). The Danger of Deconsolidation The Struggle Over Term Limits in Africa Delegative Democracy Revisited. *Journal of Democracy*, 27 (3). www.journalofdemocracy.org/sites/default/files/Foa%26Mounk-27-3.pdf

14 Brehm, Jack W. (1966). *A Theory of Psychological Reactance*. Oxford: Academic Press.

15 Kramer, A. D. I., Guillory, J. E. and Hancock, J. T. (2014). Experimental Evidence of Massive-Scale Emotional Contagion Through Social Networks. *Proceedings of the National Academy of Sciences of the United States of America*, 111 (24), 8788–8790.

16 Johnson, Clay (2014). In the wake of both the Snowden stuff and the Cuba twitter stuff, the Facebook "transmission of anger" experiment is terrifying. @cjoh, June 28.

17 Meyer, Robinson (2014). Everything We Know About Facebook's Secret Mood Manipulation Experiment. *Atlantic*, June 28. www.theatlantic.com/technology/archive/2014/06/everything-we-know-about-facebooks-secret-mood-manipulation-experiment/373648

18 Booth, Robert (2014). Facebook Reveals News Feed Experiment to Control Emotions. *Guardian*, June 29. www.theguardian.com/technology/2014/jun/29/facebook-users-emotions-news-feeds

19 Goel, Vindu (2014). Facebook Tinkers with Users' Emotions in News Feed Experiment, Stirring Outcry. *New York Times*, August 30. www.nytimes.com/2014/06/30/technology/facebook-tinkers-with-users-emotions-in-news-feed-experiment-stirring-outcry.html

20 Taylor, Charles (1991). *The Malaise of Modernity*. Toronto: House of Anansi.

21 James, William, *Principles of Psychology*.

22 Rousseau, Jean-Jacques (1755). *A Discourse on Political Economy*.

23 Pazzanese, Christina (2017). Danger in the Internet Echo Chamber. Harvard Law Today, March 24. https://today.law.harvard.edu/danger-internet-echo-chamber/

24 Lee, E., Karimi, F., Jo, H.-H., Strohmaier, M. and Wagner, C. (2017). Homophily Explains Perception Biases in Social Networks. Research paper. https://arxiv.org/pdf/1710.08601.pdf. Thompson, Derek (2017). Everybody's in a Bubble, and that's a Problem. *Atlantic*. www.theatlantic.com/business/archive/2017/01/america-bubbles/514385/

9 The Daylight

When men yield up the privilege of thinking, the last shadow of liberty quits the horizon.

Thomas Paine, *Common Sense*

The third, and most profound, level of attention is the "daylight." By this I mean the suite of foundational capacities that enable us to define our goals and values in the first place, to "want what we want to want." When our daylight is compromised, *epistemic* distraction results. Epistemic distraction is the diminishment of underlying capacities that enable a person to define or pursue their goals: capacities essential for democracy such as reflection, memory, prediction, leisure, reasoning, and goal-setting. This is where the distractions of the attention economy most directly undermine the foundations of democracy.

Epistemic distraction can make it harder to "integrate associations across many different experiences to detect common structures across them." These commonalities "form abstractions, general principles, concepts, and symbolisms that are the medium of the sophisticated, 'big-picture' thought needed for truly long-term goals."[1] In the absence of this capacity to effectively plan one's own projects and goals, our automatic, bottom-up processes take over. Thus, at its extreme, epistemic distraction produces what Harry Frankfurt refers to as "wantonness" because it removes reflected-upon, intentional reasons for action, leaving only impulsive reasons in its wake.[2]

I call this type of distraction "epistemic" for two reasons. First, it distracts from knowledge of the world (both outer and inner) that's necessary for someone to be able to function as a purposeful, competent agent. Second, it constitutes what the philosopher Miranda Fricker calls an "epistemic injustice," in that it harms a person in their ability to be a "knower" (in this case, a knower of both the world and of oneself).[3] Like existential distraction, epistemic distraction also has an impact on both autonomy and dignity. It violates the integrity of the self by undermining the necessary preconditions for it to exist and to thrive, thus pulling the carpet out from under one's feet, so to speak.

Our daylight may be obscured when our capacities for knowing what's true, or for predicting what's likely to be true, are undermined. The undermining of truth can happen via the phenomenon of "fake news," which Collins Dictionary selected as its 2017 Word of the Year, defining it as "false, often sensational, information disseminated under the guise of news reporting."[4] An Oxford University study found that during the 2016 US election, Twitter users posted more "misinformation, polarizing and conspiratorial content" than real news articles.[5] The Pope has gone so far as to call fake news a "grave sin that hurts the heart of the journalist and hurts others."[6] Our capacities for prediction may also be undermined by the attention economy, for instance when the practice of statistical opinion polling itself becomes subjugated to its incentives. Especially during major elections, it now seems that small, meaningless day-to-day changes in candidates' probabilities of winning serve as the "rewards" drawing readers back to websites whose ultimate aim is to garner page views and clicks. (When this effect occurs by design, perhaps we could call it "statbait," or statistical clickbait.)

Our daylight can also be obscured via the diminishment of intelligence or other cognitive capacities. A Hewlett-Packard study found that distractions decreased the IQ scores of knowledge workers by 10 points, which the researchers note is "twice the decline recorded for those smoking marijuana."[7] Similarly, researchers at the University of Texas found that the mere presence of one's smartphone can adversely affect available working memory capacity and functional fluid intelligence.[8] Also of relevance here are physiological effects, such as the stress produced by "email apnea," a phenomenon that occurs when a person opens their email inbox to find many unread messages, inducing a "fight-or-flight" response that causes the person to stop breathing.[9] In addition, recent research has also associated social media usage with increased social anxiety, depression, and lower mood.[10] Another source of anxiety is the phenomenon of "cyberchondria," which is defined as the "unfounded escalation of concerns about common symptomatology, based on the review of search results and literature on the Web." A 2009 study found that escalatory terminology on the pages users visit – which serves, as do clickbait headlines, to increase page views and other engagement metrics – plays a key role in this process.[11]

Reflection is an essential ingredient for the kind of thinking that helps us determine "what we want to want." For the American philosopher Christine Korsgaard, reflection is the way we "turn our attention on to our own mental activities" in order to "call our beliefs and motives into question."[12] When the technologies of our attention inhibit our capacities for reflection, our "daylight" gets obscured in ways that have particular implications for politics. For instance, notifications or addictive mobile apps may fill up those little moments in the day during which a person might have otherwise reflected on their goals and priorities. Users check their phones an average of 150 times per day[13] (and *touch* them over 2,600 times per day),[14] so that would add up to a lot of potential reflection going unrealized.

Closely related to the task of reflection is the activity of leisure. We often conflate leisure with entertainment. However, properly understood, leisure is akin to what Aristotle called "periodic non-thought".[15] It's that unstructured downtime that serves as the ground out of which one's true self bubbles forth. This sort of unstructured thought is of particular developmental importance for children.[16] The philosopher Josef Pieper even argued in 1948 that leisure is "the basis of culture," the unconscious ground out of which not only individual but also collective values and meaning-making processes emerge.[17]

Leisure also uniquely enables the kind of thinking and deliberation necessary for the thoughtful invention of societal institutions.

The philosopher Hannah Arendt saw this as being particularly true when it comes to the design of democratic systems worth having.[18] In an unpublished lecture, she writes about the authors of the United States' institutions of government:

> No doubt, it is obvious and of great consequence that this passion for freedom for its own sake awoke in and was nourished by men of leisure, by the *hommes de lettres* who had no masters and were not always busy making a living. In other words, they enjoyed the privileges of Athenian and Roman citizens without taking part in those affairs of state that so occupied the freemen of antiquity. Needless to add, where men live in truly miserable conditions this passion for freedom is unknown.[19]

"Leisure" here for Arendt seems to mean more than just "non-thought" or reflection: in counterposing it with work, she seems to be using the term to refer to something like a respite from having to perform attentional labor. A line from Theodore Roethke's 1963 poem "Infirmity" comes to mind: "A mind too active is no mind at all / The deep eye sees the shimmer on the stone ..." The busy demands of making a living can make a mind too active, but so can the busy demands of notifications, never-ending feeds of information, persuasive appeals, endless entertainment options, and all the other pings on our attention that the digital attention economy throws our way. This seems to suggest that there's an opportunity to clarify where and how our interactions with the forces of the attention economy could be considered a kind of attentional labor, and what the implications of that characterization might be for the kinds of freedom we look to leisure to sustain.

However, the most visible and consequential form of compromised "daylight" we see in the digital attention economy today is the prevalence and centrality of moral outrage. Moral outrage consists of more than just anger: it also includes the impulse to judge, punish, and shame someone you think has crossed a moral line. You're most likely to experience moral outrage when you feel not merely *angry* about some perceived misdeed, but angry and *disgusted*.[20]

Moral outrage played a useful role earlier in human evolution, when people lived in small nomadic groups: it enabled greater accountability, cooperation, and in-group trust.[21] However, the amplification of moral outrage on a societal, or even global, scale carries dire implications for the pursuit of politics worth having. In the past, when we lived in environments of information scarcity, all the world's moral transgressions weren't competing for our attention every day. According to a study in the US and Canada, less than 5 percent of the population will ever personally experience a truly moral misdeed in real life.[22] However, in the era of smartphones, if *anyone* experiences a misdeed, then *everyone* potentially experiences it.

On an almost daily basis now, it seems the entire internet – that is to say, *we* – erupt in outrage at some perceived moral transgression whose news has cascaded across the web, or gone "viral." Virality, the mass transmission of some piece of information across a network, is biased toward certain types of information over others. Since the 1960s, it's been widely held that bad news spreads more quickly and easily than good news.[23] More recent research building upon this idea has shown that it's not only the emotional "valence" of the information – namely, how good or bad it makes you feel – that influences whether or not you'll share it, but also the degree to which the particular emotion you experience produces an "arousal response" in you, namely makes you more physiologically alert and attentive.[24] In other words, if you've got two equally "bad" pieces of news to share with your friends, one of which makes you feel sad and the other angry – but you only want to share one of them – then odds are you'll share the one that angers you, because anger's a high-arousal emotion whereas sadness is low-arousal.

Here's just one example of the kind of webwide outrage cascade I'm talking about. In July of 2015 a dentist from the US state of Minnesota went hunting in Zimbabwe and killed a well-known lion named Cecil. Cecil's cause of death was an arrow followed by – after about forty hours of stumbling around, bleeding, in the wilderness – a rifle round. Cecil was then decapitated and flown to Minnesota as the trophy of a victorious hunt. It cost around $50,000 to kill Cecil. It may not have been legal.

When the story of Cecil's demise went "viral," the whole internet seemed to roar in outrage all at once. On Twitter, Cecil's memorial hashtag, #CecilTheLion, received 670,000 tweets in just twenty-four hours.[25] Comedian Jimmy Kimmel called the Minnesotan dentist "the most hated man in America who never advertised Jell-O on television." Actress Mia Farrow tweeted the dentist's address.[26] Crowds appeared at his office to yell "Murderer! Terrorist!" through megaphones and to display homemade signs suggesting that he "ROT IN HELL." Someone spray-painted "Lion Killer" on his house. Someone else took down his professional website. Still others, sitting elsewhere in the world, spent hours falsifying one-star Yelp reviews of his dental practice. On Facebook, the thousand-plus member group that emerged as the de facto mission control for Cecil's revenge brigade was called "Shame Lion Killer Dr. Walter Palmer and River Bluff Dental."[27]

When children behave like this toward one another, we use words like "cyberbullying" or "harassment." Yet when it's adults doing the shaming and threatening, we're inclined to shrug our shoulders, or even cheer it as "karma," "sweet, sweet revenge," or "justice in the court of public opinion." But it isn't any of those things. It's nothing more – and nothing less – than mob rule, a digital Salem. And today, because the targets of moral outrage can no longer be burned at the stake (in most places), the implicit goal becomes to destroy them symbolically, reputationally – we might even say *attentionally* – for their transgression.

Yet don't some transgressions *deserve* anger, and even outrage? Certainly. As the famous bumper sticker says: "if you're not outraged, you're not paying attention." Sometimes, the social pressure that comes from moral outrage is the only means we have to hold people accountable for their actions, especially when the institutions of society have failed to do so. For example, in 2011 moral outrage in Egypt led to the ouster of Hosni Mubarak from the presidency and advanced the Arab Spring.[28] In 2012 in the United States, after the shooting of Trayvon Martin, an unarmed African American teenager, moral outrage galvanized national conversations about race, guns, and accountability in law enforcement.[29] And in 2017, moral outrage finally gave a hearing to many women whose claims about the sexual offenses of Harvey Weinstein, widely considered the most powerful man in Hollywood, had previously been ignored if not outright disbelieved. Upon Weinstein's exile from the entertainment industry, similar claims came to light about other figures in Hollywood and beyond, ultimately leading to widespread societal reflection about issues of sexual harassment, gender relations, and power dynamics in the workplace.[30]

But if justice is our goal – as it should be – then it is not at all clear that these dynamics of moral outrage and mob rule advance it. If anything, they seem to lead in the opposite direction.

In her book *Anger and Forgiveness*, Martha Nussbaum describes the ways in which anger is morally problematic. She uses Aristotle's definition of anger, which is pretty close to the concept of moral outrage I gave above: it's "a desire accompanied by pain for an imagined retribution on account of an imagined slighting inflicted by people who have no legitimate reason to slight oneself or one's own." The "imagined slighting" and "imagined retribution," Nussbaum says, essentially take the form of status downrankings. She argues that much moralistic behavior, therefore, aims not at *justice*-oriented but *status*-oriented outcomes. For example, virtue signaling often masquerades as apparently useful or prudent actions, as when people take action to ensure that sex offenders don't move to their neighborhood. The real goal here, says Nussbaum, is one of "lowering the status of sex offenders and raising the status of good people like herself."

There is, however, one particular type of anger that Nussbaum views as valuable: what she calls "transition anger." This refers to anger that is followed by "the Transition," or the "healthy segue into forward-looking thoughts of welfare, and, accordingly, from anger into compassionate hope." "In a sane and not excessively anxious and status-focused person," she writes, "anger's idea of retribution or payback is a brief dream or cloud, soon dispelled by saner thoughts of personal and social welfare." However, in the attention economy, outrage cascades in such a way that the "Transition" rarely, if ever, has any chance to occur. What results, then, is unbridled mobocracy, or mob rule.

One might object here and say that "mob justice" is better than no justice at all. Nussbaum would seem to disagree: "when there is great injustice," she says, "we should not use that fact as an excuse for childish and undisciplined behavior." And while "accountability expresses society's commitment to important values," it "does not require the magical thinking of payback." In other words, recognizing that killing Cecil the Lion was the wrong thing to do, and holding those involved accountable, in no way requires – or justifies – the status-downranking behaviors of shaming or trying to destroy their reputations and livelihoods.

In 1838 a young Abraham Lincoln gave a speech at the Lyceum in Springfield, Illinois in which he warned about the threat that outrage and the mobocratic impulses it engenders pose for democracy and justice:

> [T]here is, even now, something of ill-omen, amongst us. I mean the increasing disregard for law which pervades the country; the growing disposition to substitute the wild and furious passions, in lieu of the sober judgment of Courts; and the worse than savage mobs, for the executive ministers of justice ... Thus, then, by the operation of this mobocratic spirit, which all must admit, is now abroad in the land, the strongest bulwark of any Government, and particularly of those constituted like ours, may effectually be broken down and destroyed.[31]

He continued: "There is no grievance that is a fit object of redress by mob law." Mobocratic "justice" is no justice worth having, and this is only partly because of the outcomes it tends to produce. It's also because of the *way* mobocracy goes about producing them.

Legal professionals have a saying: "Justice is the process, not the outcome."[32] The process of mobocratic "justice" fueled by viral outrage that cascades online is one of caprice, arbitrariness, and uncertainty. So it should come as no surprise that mob rule is precisely the path that Socrates, in *The Republic*, describes as being the path societies take from democracy back into tyranny.[33]

Unfortunately, mob rule is hard-coded into the design of the attention economy. In this way, it can be considered a kind of society-wide utility function that optimizes for extremism, which may at times even manifest as terrorism. It creates an environment in which extremist actors, causes, or groups who feed on outrage can flourish. As the writer Tobias Rose-Stockwell has put it, "this is the uncomfortable truth of terrorism's prominence in our lives: We have built an instant distribution system for its actual intent – *Terror*."[34]

On an individual level, the proliferation of outrage creates more fear and anxiety in our lives. A headline of an article on the satirical news site The Onion reads, "Blogger Takes Few Moments Every Morning To Decide Whether To Feel Outraged, Incensed, Or Shocked By Day's News."[35] It also contributes to the "stickiness," or the compulsive effects of the medium, that keep us "hooked" and continually coming back for more. It can also skew our view of the world by giving us the impression that things are much worse than they actually are. In his essay *A Free Man's Worship*, Bertrand Russell writes, "indignation is still a bondage, for it compels our thoughts to be occupied with an evil world; and in the fierceness of desire from which rebellion springs there is a kind of self-assertion which it is necessary for the wise to overcome."[36] Or, as a worker in a Russian "troll house" put it, "if every day you are feeding on hate, it eats away at your soul."[37]

When the attention economy amplifies moral outrage in a way that moralizes political division, it clears the way for the tribalistic impulse to claim for one's own group the mantle of representing the "real" or "true" will of the people as a whole. This, for Jan-Werner Müller in *What is Populism?*, is the essence of the concept of "populism."[38]

In recent years we've witnessed a flood of political events across Western liberal democracies that have been described as "populist" in character. Yet the term's definition has remained stubbornly mercurial. Some have used it to refer to particularly emotive styles of collective action. Some have used it to mean antielitism, others antipluralism. And some simply use it to describe a type of politics that seems vaguely problematic. Our conceptions of populism have themselves been polarized.

Müller offers a helpful corrective. In his book, he writes that populism is "a particular *moralistic imagination of politics*, a way of perceiving the political world that sets a morally pure and fully unified ... people against elites who are deemed corrupt or in some other way morally inferior." He says that "populism is about making a certain kind of moral claim," namely that "only some of the people are really the people." In *The Social Contract*, Rousseau warned of the risk that "particular wills could replace the general will in the deliberations of the people." Müller's conception of populism can thus be seen as a kind of moralized version of that fragmentation of collective identity. But while the development of Rousseau's general will "requires actual participation by citizens; the populist, on the other hand, can divine the proper will of the people on the basis of what it means, for instance, to be a 'real American.'"

The work of Berkeley cognitive linguist George Lakoff is extremely relevant here. For several years he has been calling attention to the way in which American politics may be read as the projection of family systems dynamics onto the body politic: in this reading, the right is the "strict father" whereas the left is the "nurturing mother."[39] (It is relevant here to note that in 2004, one of the highest-correlated views with voting Republican was support for corporal punishment, or "spanking" one's children.)[40] Lakoff explains, "the basic idea is that authority is justified by morality, and that, in a well-ordered world, there should be a moral hierarchy in which those who have traditionally dominated should dominate." He continues, "The hierarchy is God above man; man above nature; the rich above the poor; employers above employees; adults above children; Western culture above other cultures; our country above other countries. The hierarchy also extends to men above women, whites above non-whites, Christians above non-Christians, straights above gays." "Since this is seen as a 'natural' order," he continues, "it is not to be questioned."[41]

It's easy to spot examples of populism, on this particular definition, across the political spectrum in recent years. On the right, it manifests as appeals to rural American voters as being "real Americans," "birtherism," or Nigel Farage's hailing of the UK's "Brexit" vote as a "victory for real people." On the left, it manifests as appeals to "the 99%" (i.e. we are "the people," if you round up), as well as in various manifestations of identity politics.

Müller writes that populists "can accurately be described as 'enemies of institutions' – although not of institutions in general" – only "mechanisms of representation that fail to vindicate their claim to exclusive moral representation." In this light, calls on the American left in the wake of the 2016 US presidential election to abolish the electoral college system (in which Hillary Clinton lost the electoral vote but won the popular vote) may be read as similarly "impulsive" desires to get rid of intermediary regulatory systems. "Everything that liberals from Montesquieu and Tocqueville onward once lauded as moderating influences – what they called intermediate institutions – disappears here in favor of Urbinati's 'direct representation.'"

Importantly, Müller also writes that political crises don't cause populism: "a crisis – whether economic, social, or ultimately also political – does not automatically produce populism" of this sort. Nor can populism merely be chalked up to "frustration," "anger," or "resentment" – to take such a view would not only be uncharitable but indeed also patronizing, and even a dereliction of one's duties as a citizen. As Müller writes, "simply to shift the discussion to social psychology (and treat the angry and frustrated as potential patients for a political sanatorium) is to neglect a basic democratic duty to engage in reasoning."

Yet the technologies of the digital attention economy don't promote or select for the kind of reasoning, deliberation, or understanding that's necessary to take political action beyond the white-hot flash of outrage and revolution. As Wael Ghonim, the Egyptian activist who set up the Facebook group that was instrumental in sparking the Arab Spring, said in a talk called "The Algorithms of Fear":

> We who use the Internet now "like" or we flame – but there's [very little] now happening [algorithmically] to drive people into the more consensus-based, productive discussions we need to have, to help us make civic progress. Productive discussions aren't getting the [media] distribution they deserve. We're not driving people to content that could help us, as a society ... come together without a flame war ... You can build algorithms and experiences that are designed to get the best out of people, and you can build algorithms and experiences that drive out the worst. It's our job as civic technologists to build experiences that drive the best. We can do that. We must do that now.[42]

What's the best part of people that our technologies should be designed to bring out? What should the system be inducing in us instead of outrage? Nussbaum writes, "the spirit that should be our goal has many names: Greek *philophrosunē*, Roman *humanitas*, biblical *agapē*, African *ubuntu* – a patient and forbearing disposition to see and seek the good rather than to harp obsessively on the bad."

The problem, of course, is that the "patient and forbearing disposition to see and seek the good" does not grab eyeballs, and therefore does not sell ads. "Harping obsessively on the bad," however, does. As it stands, the dynamics of the attention economy are thus structurally set up to undermine the most noble aims and virtues worth pursuing. Again, outrage and anger are not bad – they are understandable human responses to injustice, and they can even make us feel happy, in a way.[43] However, because the attention economy contains many incentives to induce anger but none to induce the "Transition," outrage rapidly cascades into mobocracy on a societal, if not global, scale.

By compromising the "daylight" of our attention, then, the digital attention economy directly militates against the foundations of democracy and justice. It undermines fundamental capacities that are preconditions for self-determination at both the individual and the collective level. In fact, to the extent that we take these fundamental capacities to be among our uniquely human guiding lights, there's a very real sense in which epistemic distraction *literally* dehumanizes.

NOTES

1 Miller, Earl K. and Buschman, Timothy J. (2014). Natural Mechanisms for the Executive Control of Attention. *The Oxford Handbook of Attention*, ed. Anna C. Nobre and Sabine Kastner. Oxford University Press.

2 Frankfurt, Harry G. (1988). *The Importance of What We Care About: Philosophical Essays*. Cambridge University Press.

3 Fricker, Miranda (2007). *Epistemic Injustice: Power and the Ethics of Knowing*. Oxford University Press.

4 Collins Dictionary (2017). Collins Dictionary Word of the Year. www.collinsdictionary.com/woty

5 Howard, P. N., Kollanyi, B., Bradshaw, S. and Neudert, L. M. (2017). Social Media, News and Political Information During the US Election: Was Polarizing Content Concentrated in Swing States? Data memo, Oxford Internet Institute. http://comprop.oii.ox.ac.uk/wp-content/uploads/sites/89/2017/09/Polarizing-Content-and-Swing-States.pdf

6 Associated Press (2017). Pope Francis: Fake and Sensationalised News "A Very Serious Sin." *Guardian*, December 17.

www.theguardian.com/world/2017/dec/17/pope-francis-fake-and-sensationalised-news-a-very-serious-sin

7 Hemp, Paul (2009). Death by Information Overload. *Harvard Business Review*, September. https://hbr.org/2009/09/death-by-information-overload

8 Ward, A. F., Duke, K., Gneezy, A. and Bos, M. W. (2017). Brain Drain: The Mere Presence of One's Own Smartphone Reduces Available Cognitive Capacity. *Journal of the Association for Consumer Research*, 2 (2), 140–154.

9 Stone, Linda (2008). Just Breathe: Building the Case for Email Apnea. Huffington Post blog. www.huffingtonpost.com/linda-stone/just-breathe-building-the_b_85651.html

10 Kross, E. et al. (2013). Facebook Use Predicts Declines in Subjective Well-being in Young Adults. *PLoS ONE*, 8 (8), 1–6. Lin, L. Y. et al. (2016). Association Between Social Media Use and Depression Among U.S. Young Adults. *Depress Anxiety*, 33 (4), 323–331. Ryan, Tracii and Xenos, Sophia (2011). Who Uses Facebook? An Investigation Into the Relationship Between the Big Five, Shyness, Narcissism, Loneliness, and Facebook Usage. *Computers in Human Behavior*, 27 (5), 1658–1664. Sagioglou, Christina and Greitemeyer, Tobias (2014). Facebook's Emotional Consequences: Why Facebook Causes a Decrease in Mood and Why People Still Use It. *Computers in Human Behavior*, 35, 359–363.

11 White, Ryen and Horvitz, Eric (2009). Cyberchondria: Studies of the Escalation of Medical Concerns in Web Search. *ACM Transactions on Information Systems (TOIS)* 27 (4), 23.

12 Korsgaard, Christine M. (1996). *The Sources of Normativity*. Cambridge University Press.

13 Ahonen T. (2013). The Mobile Telecoms Industry Annual Review for 2013. www.slideshare.net/kleinerperkins/kpcb-internet-trends-2013/52-Mobile_Users_Reach_to_Phone

14 dscout (2016). Mobile Touches: dscout's Inaugural Study on Humans and Their Tech. https://blog.dscout.com/hubfs/downloads /dscout_mobile_touches_study_2016.pdf

15 North, Paul (2011). *The Problem of Distraction*. Palo Alto, CA: Stanford University Press.

16 Barker, J. E. et al. (2014). Less-Structured Time in Children's Daily Lives Predicts Self-Directed Executive Functioning. *Frontiers in Psychology*, 5, 593.

17 Pieper, Josef (1948). *Leisure: The Basis of Culture and the Philosophical Act* (p. 144). San Francisco, CA: Ignatius Press.

18 Arendt, Hannah (2013). *The Human Condition*. University of Chicago Press.

19 Arendt, Hannah (unpublished). Thoughts on Poverty, Misery and the Great Revolutions of History.

20 Salerno, Jessica and Peter-Hagene, Liana (2013). The Interactive Effect of Anger and Disgust on Moral Outrage and Judgments. *Psychological Science*, August 22. http://journals.sagepub.com/doi/10.1177/0956797613486988

21 Crockett, M. J. (2017). Moral Outrage in the Digital Age. *Nature Human Behaviour*, 1 (11), 769–771. Panchanathan, Karthik and Boyd, Robert (2004). Indirect Reciprocity Can Stabilize Cooperation Without the Second-Order Free Rider Problem. *Nature*, 432 (7016), 499–502.

22 Hofmann, W., Wisneski, D. C., Brandt, M. J. and Skitka, L. J. (2014). Replication Data For Morality in Everyday Life. Harvard Dataverse.

23 Galtung, Johan and Ruge, Mari (1965). The Structure of Foreign News: The Presentation of the Congo, Cuba and Cyprus Crises in Four Norwegian Newspapers. *Journal of Peace Research*, 2 (1), 64–90.

24 Dobele, A., Lindgreen, A., Beverland, M., Vanhamme, J. and van Wijk, R. (2007). Why Pass on Viral Messages? Because They Connect Emotionally. *Business Horizons*, 50 (4), 291–304. Berger, Jonah and Milkman, Katherine L. (2011). Social Transmission, Emotion and the Virality of Online Content (1–53). Research paper, Operations, Information and Decisions Department, University of Pennsylvania. http://opim.wharton.upenn.edu/~kmilkman/Virality.pdf. Rimé, B., Philippot, P., Boca, S. and Mesquita, B. (1992). Long-lasting Cognitive and Social Consequences of Emotion: Social Sharing and Rumination. *European Review of Social Psychology*, 3 (1), 225–258.

25 Valinsky, Jordan (2015). Outrage and Backlash: #CecilTheLion Racks up 670K Tweets in 24 Hours. Digiday. https://digiday.com/marketing/outrage-backlash-cecilthelion-racks-670k-tweets-24-hours/

26 Chasmar, Jessica (2015). Mia Farrow Tweets Address of Walter Palmer, Dentist who Killed Cecil the Lion. *Washington Times*, July 29. www.washingtontimes.com/news/2015/jul/29/mia-farrow-tweets-address-of-walter-palmer-dentist/

27 Capecchi, C. and Rogers, K. (2015). Killer of Cecil the Lion Finds out that he is a Target Now, of Internet Vigilantism. *New York Times*, July 30. www.nytimes.com/2015/07/30/us/cecil-the-lion-walter-palmer.html

28 Briefing (2017). Once Considered a Boon to Democracy, Social Media Have Started to Look Like its Nemesis. *Economist*, November 4. www.economist .com/news/briefing/21730870-economy-based-attention-easily-gamed-once-considered-boon-democracy-social-media

29 #BlackLivesMatter Campaign. http://blacklivesmatter.com/

30 #metoo Campaign. https://twitter.com/hashtag/metoo. BBC Entertainment and Arts (2017). Harvey Weinstein Timeline: How the Scandal Unfolded. www.bbc.com/news/entertainment-arts-41594672

31 Lincoln, Abraham (1838). The Perpetuation of our Political Institutions: Address Before the Young Men's Lyceum of Springfield, Illinois. www.abrahamlincolnonline.org/lincoln/speeches/lyceum.htm

32 Kolkey, Daniel M. (1993). Justice is in the Process, not Outcome: The Racially Mixed Jury in the King Civil-Rights Trial is One Sign that the System Works. *LA Times*, March 9. http://articles.latimes.com/1993-03-09/local/me-991_1_jury-selection-process

33 Plato, *Republic*.

34 Rose-Stockwell, Tobias (2017). This is How your Fear and Outrage are Being Sold for Profit. The Mission, July 14. https://medium.com/the-mission/the-enemy-in-our-feeds-e86511488de

35 The Onion (2015). Blogger Takes Few Moments Every Morning to Decide Whether to Feel Outraged, Incensed, or Shocked by Day's News. www.theonion.com/blogger-takes-few-moments-every-morning-to-decide-wheth-1819578040

36 Russell, Bertrand (1903). A Free Man's Worship. www.philosophicalsociety .com/archives/a%20free%20man's%20worship.htm

37 Walker, Shaun (2015). Salutin' Putin: Inside a Russian Troll House. *Guardian*, April 2. www.theguardian.com/world/2015/apr/02/putin-kremlin-inside-russian-troll-house

38 Müller, Jan-Werner (2016). *What is Populism?* Philadelphia: University of Pennsylvania Press.

39 Lakoff, G. (1996). *Moral Politics*. University of Chicago Press.

40 Rosenberg, P. (2016). Trump's Extremism has Deep GOP Roots: The Correlation Between Corporal Punishment and Voting Republican. Salon,

September 1. www.salon.com/2016/08/01/trumps_extremism_has_deep_gop_roots_the_correlation_between_corporal_punishment_and_voting_republican/

41 Lakoff, George (1996). *Moral Politics*. University of Chicago Press.

42 Stepanek, Marcia (2016). The Algorithms of Fear. *Stanford Innovation Review*, June 14. https://ssir.org/articles/entry/the_algorithms_of_fear

43 Silver, Katie (2017). Anger and Hatred can Make us Feel Happy, Says Study. BBC News. www.bbc.co.uk/news/health-40900811

III Freedom of Attention

10 The Ground of First Struggle

Technology means constant social revolution.

Marshall McLuhan, *The Mechanical Bride*

Language has a curious way of sticking around. We still say "the sun rises," even though we know it is we who turn into the sun. So it shouldn't surprise us that we've inherited the largest, most powerful, and most centralized infrastructure for shaping thought and behavior in human history, but we still haven't gotten around to calling it what it is. We persist in describing these systems as "information" or "communication" technologies, despite the fact that they are, by and large, designed neither to inform us nor help us communicate – at least in any way that's recognizably human. We beat our breasts about "fake news" and other varieties of onerous content because it's easier than taking aim at the fundamental problems with the medium itself: that it's an answer to a question no one ever asked, that its goals are not our goals, that it's a machine designed to harvest our attention wantonly and in wholesale.

The proliferation of ubiquitous, portable, and connected general-purpose computers has enabled this infrastructure of industrialized persuasion to do an end run around all other societal systems and to open a door directly onto our attentional faculties, on which it now operates for over a third of our waking lives. In the hands of a few dozen people now lies the power to shape the attentional habits – the *lives* – of billions of human beings. This is not a situation in which the essential political problem involves the management or censorship of speech. The total effect of these systems on our lives is not analogous to that of past communications media. The effect here is much closer to that of a religion: it's the installation of a worldview, the habituation into certain practices and values, the appeals to tribalistic impulses, the hypnotic abdication of reason and will, and the faith in these omnipresent and seemingly omniscient forces that we trust, without a sliver of verification, to be on our side.

This fierce competition for human attention is creating new problems of kind, not merely of degree. Via ubiquitous and always connected interfaces to users, as well as a sophisticated infrastructure of measurement, experimentation, targeting, and analytics, this global project of industrialized persuasion is now the dominant business model and design logic of the internet. To date, the problems of "distraction" have been minimized as minor annoyances. Yet the competition for attention and the "persuasion" of users ultimately amounts to a project of the manipulation of the will. We currently lack a language for talking about, and thereby recognizing, the full depth of these problems. At individual levels, these problems threaten to frustrate one's authorship of one's own life. At collective levels, they threaten to frustrate the authorship of the story of a people and obscure the common interests and goals that bind them together, whether that group is a family, a community, a country, or all of humankind. In a sense, these societal systems have been short-circuited. In doing so, the operation of the will – which is the basis of the authority of politics – has also been short-circuited and undermined.

Uncritical deployment of the human-as-computer metaphor is today the well of a vast swamp of irrelevant prognostications about the human future. If people *were* computers, however, the appropriate description of the digital attention economy's incursions upon their processing capacities would be that of the distributed denial-of-service, or DDoS, attack. In a DDoS attack, the attacker controls many computers and uses them to send many repeated requests to the target computer, effectively overwhelming its capacity to communicate with any other computer. The competition to monopolize our attention is like a DDoS attack against the human will.

In fact, to the extent that the attention economy seeks to achieve the capture and exploitation of human desires, actions, decisions, and ultimately lives, we may view it as a type of human trafficking. A 2015 report funded by the European Commission called "The Onlife Manifesto" does just that: "To the same extent that organs should not be exchanged on the market place, our attentional capabilities deserve protective treatment ... in addition to offering informed choices, the default settings and other designed aspects of our technologies should respect and protect attentional capabilities." The report calls for paying greater attention "to attention itself as a [sic] inherent human attribute that conditions the flourishing of human interactions and the capabilities to engage in meaningful action."[1]

Today, as in Huxley's time, we have "failed to take into account" our "almost infinite appetite for distractions."[2] The effect of the global attention economy – that is, of many of our digital technologies doing precisely what they are designed to do – is to frustrate and even erode the human will at individual and collective levels, undermining the very assumptions of democracy. They guide us and direct us, but they do not fulfill us or sustain us. These are the "distractions" of a system that is not on our side.

These are our new empires of the mind, and our present relation with them is one of attentional serfdom. Rewiring this relationship is a "political" task in two ways. First, because our media are the lens through which we understand and engage with those matters we have historically understood as "political." Second, because they are now the lens through which we view *everything*, including ourselves. "The most complete authority," Rousseau wrote in *A Discourse on Political Economy*, "is the kind that penetrates the inner man, and influences his will as much as his actions" (p. 13). This is the kind of authority that our information technologies – these technologies of our attention – now have over us. As a result, we ought to understand them as the ground of first political struggle, the politics behind politics. It is now impossible to achieve any political reform worth having without first reforming the totalistic forces that guide our attention and our lives.

Looking to the future, the trajectory is one of ever greater power of the digital attention economy over our lives. More of our day-to-day experience stands to be mediated and guided by smaller, faster, more ubiquitous, more intelligent, and more engaging entry points into the digital attention economy. As Marc Andreessen, an investor and the author of Mosaic, the first web browser I ever used, said in 2011, "Software is eating the world."[3] In addition, the amount of monetizable attention in our lives is poised to increase substantially if technologies such as driverless vehicles, or economic policies such as Universal Basic Income, come to fruition and increase our amount of available leisure time.

Persuasion may also prove to be the "killer app" for artificial intelligence, or AI. The mantra "AI is the new UI" is informing much of the next generation interface design currently under way (e.g. Apple's Siri, Amazon's Alexa, or Google Home), and the more that the vision of computing as intelligent, frictionless assistance becomes reality, the more the logic and values of the system will be pushed below the surface of awareness to the automation layer and rendered obscure to users, or to any others who might want to question their design. Already, our most common interactions with some of the most sophisticated AI systems in history occur in contexts of persuasion, and the application of AI in so-called "programmatic" advertising is expected to accelerate.[4] One major reason for this is that advertising is where many of the near term business interests lie. Much of the cutting edge of AI research and development now takes place within the walls of companies whose primary business model is advertising – and so, having this existing profit motive to serve, it's only natural that their first priority would be to apply their innovations toward growing their business. For example, one of the first projects that Google's DeepMind division put their "AlphaGo" system to work on was enhancing YouTube's video recommendation algorithm.[5] In other words, it now seems the same intelligence behind the system that defeated the human world champion at the game Go is sitting on the other side of your screen and showing you videos that it thinks will keep you using YouTube for as long as possible.

Yet the affinity between advertising and AI extends well beyond the incidental fact that advertising is the current business context in which much leading AI development today occurs. In particular, the problem space of advertising is an extremely good fit for the capabilities of AI: it combines a mind-boggling multiplicity of inputs (e.g. contextual, behavioral, and other user signals) with the laserlike specificity of a clear, binary goal (i.e. typically the purchase, or "conversion," as it's often called). Perhaps this is why games have been the other major domain in which artificial intelligence has been tested and innovated. On a conceptual level, training an algorithm to play chess or an Atari 2600 game well is quite similar to training an algorithm to advertise well. Both involve training an agent that interacts with its environment to grapple with an enormous amount of unstructured data and take actions based on that data to maximize expected rewards as represented by a single variable.

Perhaps an intuition about this affinity between advertising and algorithmic automation lay behind that almost mystic comment of McLuhan's in *Understanding Media*:

> To put the matter abruptly, the advertising industry is a crude attempt to extend the principles of automation to every aspect of society. Ideally, advertising aims at the goal of a programmed harmony among all human impulses and aspirations and endeavors. Using handicraft methods, it stretches out toward the ultimate electronic goal of a collective consciousness. When all production and all consumption are brought into a pre-established harmony with all desire and all effort, then advertising will have liquidated itself by its own success.[6]

It's probably not useful, or even possible, to ask what McLuhan got "right" or "wrong" here: in keeping with his style, the observation is best read as a "probe." Regardless, it seems clear that he's making two erroneous assumptions about advertising: (1) that the advertising system, or any of its elements, has "harmony" as a goal; and (2) that human desire is a finite quantity merely to be balanced against other system dynamics. On the contrary, since the inception of modern advertising we have seen it continually seek not only to fulfill existing desires, but also to generate new ones; not only to meet people's needs and demands, but to produce more where none previously existed. McLuhan seems to view advertising as a closed system which, upon reaching a certain threshold of automation, settles into a kind of socioeconomic homeostasis, reaching a plateau of sufficiency via the (apparently unregulated) means of efficiency. Of course, as long as advertising remains aimed at the ends of continual growth, its tools of efficiency are unlikely to optimize for anything like sufficiency or systemic harmony. Similarly, as long as some portion of human life manages to confound advertising's tools of prediction – which I suggest will always be the case – it is unlikely to *be able* to optimize for a total systemic harmony. This is a very good thing, because it lets us dispense at the outset with imagined, abstracted visions of "automation" as a generalized type of force (or, even more broadly, "algorithms"), and focus instead on the particular instances of automation that actually present themselves to us, the most advanced implementations of which we currently find on the battlefield of digital advertising.

Looking forward, the technologies of the digital attention economy are also poised to know us ever more intimately, in order to persuade us ever more effectively. Already, over 250 Android mobile device games listen to sounds from users' environments.[7] This listening may one day even extend to our inner environments. In 2015, Facebook filed a patent for detecting emotions, both positive and negative, from computer and smartphone cameras.[8] And in April 2017, at the company's F8 conference, Facebook researcher Regina Dugan, a former head of DARPA (the US Defense Advanced Research Projects Agency), took the stage to discuss the company's development of a brain–computer interface.[9]

Dugan stresses that it's not about invading your thoughts – an important disclaimer, given the public's anxiety over privacy violations from social network's [sic] as large as Facebook. Rather, "this is about decoding the words you've already decided to share by sending them to the speech center of your brain," reads the company's official announcement. "Think of it like this: You take many photos and choose to share only some of them. Similarly, you have many thoughts and choose to share only some of them."[10]

The company refused to say whether they plan to use information collected from the speech center of your brain for advertising purposes.

We face great challenges today across the full stack of human life: at planetary, societal, organizational, and individual levels. Success in surmounting these challenges requires that we give the right sort of attention to the right sort of things. A major function, if not the primary purpose, of information technology should be to advance this end.

Yet for all its informational benefits, the rapid proliferation of digital technologies has compromised attention, in this wide sense, and produced a suite of cognitive-behavioral externalities that we are still only beginning to understand and mitigate. The enveloping of human life by information technologies has resulted in an informational environment whose dynamics the global persuasion industry has quickly come to dominate, and, in a virtually unbounded manner, has harnessed to engineer unprecedented advances in techniques of measurement, testing, automation, and persuasive design. The process continues apace, yet already we find ourselves entrusting enormous portions of our waking lives to technologies that compete with one another to maximize their share of our lives, and, indeed, to grow the stock of life that's available for them to capture.

This process will not cross any threshold of intolerability that forces us to act. It came on, and continues to evolve, gradually. There will be no voice or light from the sky showing how we've become ensconced in a global infrastructure of intelligent persuasion. There will be no scales dropping from eyes, no Toto pulling back the curtain to reveal the would-be wizards pulling their levers. There will be no sudden realization of the gravity and unsustainability of this situation.

Milton Mayer describes how such a gradual process of normalization made even living under the Third Reich feel like no big deal. In his book *They Thought They Were Free*, he writes:

> But the one great shocking occasion, when tens or hundreds or thousands will join with you, never comes. *That's* the difficulty. If the last and worst act of the whole regime had come immediately after the first and smallest, thousands, yes, millions would have been sufficiently shocked ... But of course this isn't the way it happens. In between come all the hundreds of little steps, some of them imperceptible, each of them preparing you not to be shocked by the next ... And one day, too late, your principles, if you were ever sensible of them, all rush in upon you. The burden of self-deception has grown too heavy, and some minor incident, in my case my little boy, hardly more than a baby, saying "Jewish swine," collapses it all at once, and you see that everything, everything, has changed and changed completely under your nose ... Now you live in a world of hate and fear, and the people who hate and fear do not even know it themselves; when everyone is transformed, no one is transformed ... The system itself could not have intended this in the beginning, but in order to sustain itself it was compelled to go all the way.[11]

No designer ever went into design to make people's lives worse. I don't know any software engineers or product managers who want to undermine the assumptions of democracy. I've never met a digital marketing manager who aims to make society more outraged and fearful. No one in the digital attention economy *wants* to be standing in the lights of our attention. Yet the system, in order to sustain itself, has been compelled to go all the way.

This is an intolerable situation. What, then, is to be done? Like Diogenes to Alexander, we urgently need to look up at these well-meaning Alexanders of our time and tell them to "stand out of our light." Alexander didn't know he was standing in Diogenes' light because it didn't occur to him to ask. He was focused on *his* offer and *his* goals, not Diogenes' goals or what was being obscured by his offer. In the same way, the creators of our digital technologies don't know that they're standing in our light because it doesn't occur to them to ask. They have focused on *their* goals and *their* desired effects, rather than our goals or the important "lights" in our lives they may be obscuring.

For us, responding in the right way means treating the design of digital technologies as the ground of first struggle for our freedom and self-determination: as the politics *behind* politics that shapes our attentional world and directs downstream effects according to its own ends. Yet this new form of power does not go by the usual names, it does not play by the usual rules, and indeed those who wield this power take pains to pretend – despite the strenuous cognitive dissonance of such a claim – that they are not wielding any great political power at all. Yet it is plain that they do.

Ultimately, responding in the right way also means changing the system so that these technologies are, as they already claim to be, *on our side*. It is an urgent task to bring the dynamics and constraints of the technologies of our attention into alignment with those of our political systems. This requires a sustained effort to reject the forces of attentional serfdom, and to assert and defend our freedom of attention.

NOTES

1 Floridi, Luciano (ed.) (2015). *The Onlife Manifesto*. Basle: Springer International.
2 Huxley, Aldous (1985). *Brave New World Revisited*. New York, NY: Harper & Brothers.

3 Andreesen, Marc (2011). Why Software is Eating the World. *Wall Street Journal*, August 20. www.wsj.com/articles/SB10001424053111 9034809045765122509 15629460

4 Victory, Chris (2017). In 2018, Marketers Will Discover More AI Applications in Programmatic Advertising. Emarketer. www.emarketer.com/Article/ 2018-Marketers-Will-Discover-More-AI-Applications-Programmatic-Advertising/1016801

5 Simonite, Tom (2016). How Google Plans to Solve Artificial Intelligence. *MIT Technology Review*, March 31. www.technologyreview.com/s/ 601139/how-google-plans-to-solve-artificial-intelligence/. Rowan, David (2015). DeepMind: Inside Google's Super-brain. WIRED, June 22. www .wired.co.uk/article/deepmind

6 McLuhan, Marshall (1994). *Understanding Media: The Extensions of Man.* Cambridge, MA: MIT Press.

7 Sapna, Maheshwari (2017). That Game on your Phone may be Tracking what you're Watching on TV. *New York Times*, December 28. www.nytimes .com/2017/12/28/business/media/alphonso-app-tracking.html

8 Naveh, R. N. (2014). Techniques for Emotion Detection and Content Delivery. United States Patent Application Publication. http://pdfaiw .uspto.gov/.aiw?docid=20150242679

9 Statt, Nick (2017). Facebook is Working on a Way to Let you Type with your Brain. The Verge, April 19. www.theverge.com/2017/4/19/15360798/ facebook-brain-computer-interface-ai-ar-f8-2017

10 Biddle, Sam (2017). Facebook Won't Say if it Will Use your Brain Activity for Advertisements. The Intercept, May 22. https://theintercept.com/ 2017/05/22/facebook-wont-say-if-theyll-use-your-brain-activity-for-advertisements/

11 Mayer, Milton (1955). *They Thought They Were Free.* University of Chicago Press, pp. 170–171.

11   The Monster and the Bank

A perceptive and critical reader may object here that I've given too much airtime to the *problems* of the digital attention economy and not enough to its *benefits*. They would be quite right. This is by design. "Why?" they might ask. "Shouldn't we make an even-handed assessment of these technologies, and fully consider their benefits along with their costs? Shouldn't we take care not to throw out the baby with the bath water?"

No, we should not. To proceed in that way would grant the premise that it's acceptable for our technologies to be adversarial against us to begin with. It would serve as implicit agreement that we'll tolerate design that isn't on our side, as long as it throws us a few consolation prizes along the way. But adversarial technology is not even worthy of the name "technology." And I see no reason, either moral or practical, why we should be expected to tolerate it. If anything, I see good reasons for thinking it morally obligatory that we resist and reform it. Silver linings are the consolations of the disempowered, and I refuse to believe that we are in that position relative to our technologies yet.

The reader might also object, "Are any of these dynamics *really* new at all? Does the digital attention economy *really* pose a fundamentally new threat to human freedom?" To be sure, incentives to capture and hold people's attention existed long before digital technologies arose: elements of the attention economy have been present in previous electric media, such as radio and television, and even further back we find in the word "claptrap" a nice eighteenth-century analogue of "clickbait." It's also true that our psychological biases get exploited all the time: when a supermarket sets prices that end in .99, when a software company buries a user-hostile stipulation in a subordinate clause on page 97 of their terms-of-service agreement, or when a newspaper requires you to call, rather than email, in order to cancel your subscription. However, these challenges *are* new: as I have already argued here, this persuasion is far more powerful and prevalent than ever before, its pace of change is faster than ever before, and it's centralized in the hands of fewer people than ever before.

This is a watershed moment on the trajectory of divesting our media, that is to say our attentional world, of the biases of print media, a trajectory that arguably has been in motion since the telegraph. But this process is more exponential than it is linear, tracking as it does the rate of technology change as a whole. The fact that this can be placed on an existing trajectory means it is *more* important, not less, to address.

It's also wrongheaded to say that taking action to reform the digital attention economy would be premature because we lack sufficient clarity about the precise causal relationships between particular designs and particular types of harm. We will *never* have the sort of "scientific" clarity about the effects of digital media that we have, say, about the effects of the consumption of different drugs. The technology is changing too fast for research to keep up, its users and their contexts are far too diverse to allow anything but the broadest generalizations as conclusions, and the relationships between people and digital technologies are far too complex to make most research of this nature feasible at all. Again, though, the assumption behind calls to "wait and see" is that there's a scenario in which we'd be willing to accept design that is adversarial against us in the first place. To demand randomized controlled trials, or similarly rigorous modes of research, before setting out to rewire the attention economy is akin to demanding verification that the opposing army marching toward you do, indeed, have bullets in their guns.

Additionally, it's important to be very clear about what I'm *not* claiming here. For one, my argument is in no way anti technology or anti commerce. This is no Luddite move. The perspective I take, and the suggestions I will make, are in no way incompatible with making money, nor do they constitute a "brake pedal" on technological innovation. They're more of a "steering wheel." Ultimately, this is a project that takes seriously the claim, and helps advance the vision, that technology design can "make the world a better place."

Also, it's important to reiterate that I'm not arguing our non-rational psychological biases are in themselves "bad," nor that exploiting them via design is inherently undesirable. As I wrote earlier, doing so is inevitable, and design can greatly advance users' interests with these dynamics, when it's on their side. As Huxley writes in his 1962 novel *Island*, "we cannot argue ourselves out of our basic irrationality – we can only learn to be irrational in a reasonable way." Or, as Hegel puts it in *Philosophy of Right*, "Impulses should be phases of will in a rational system."[1]

Nor, of course, am I arguing that digital technologies somehow "rewire" our brains, or otherwise change the way we think on a physiological level. Additionally, I'm not arguing here that the main problem is that we're being "manipulated" by design. Manipulation is standardly understood as "controlling the content and supply of information" in such a way that the person is not aware of the influence. This seems to me simply another way of describing what most design *is*.

Neither does my argument require for its moral claims the presence of *addiction*.[2] It's enough to simply say that when you put people in different environments, they behave differently. There are many ways in which technology can be unethical, and can even deprive us of our freedom, without being "addictive." Those in the design community and elsewhere who adopt a default stance of defensiveness on these issues often latch on to the conceptual frame of "addiction" in order to avoid having to meaningfully engage with the implications of ethically questionable design. This may occur explicitly or implicitly (the latter often by analogy to other addiction-forming products such as alcohol, cigarettes, or sugary foods). As users, we implicitly buy into these ethically constraining frames when we use phrases such as "digital detox" or "binge watch." It's ironic that comparing our technologies to dependency-inducing chemicals would render us *less* able to hold them ethically accountable for their designs and effects – but this is precisely the case. When we do so, we give up far too much ethical ground: we help to erect a straw man argument that threatens to commandeer the wider debate about the overall alignment of technology design with human goals and values. We must not confuse clinical standards with moral standards. Whether irresistible or not, if our technologies are not on our side, then they have no place in our lives.

It's also worth noting several pitfalls we should avoid, namely things we must *not* do in response to the challenges of the attention economy. For one, we must not reply that if someone doesn't like the choices on technology's menu, their only option is to "unplug" or "detox." This is a pessimistic and unsustainable view of technology, and one at odds with its very purpose. We have neither reason nor obligation to accept a relationship with technology that is adversarial in nature.

We must also be vigilant about the risk of slipping into an overly moralistic mode. Metaphors of food, alcohol, or drugs are often (though not always) signals of such overmoralizing. A recent headline in the British newspaper *The Independent* proclaims, "Giving your Child a Smartphone is Like Giving them a Gram of Cocaine, Says Top Addiction Expert."[3] Oxford researchers Andy Przybylski and Amy Orben penned a reply to that article in The Conversation, in which they wrote,

> To fully confirm *The Independent*'s headline ... you would need to give children both a gram of cocaine and a smartphone and then compare the effects ... Media reports that compare social media to drug use are ignoring evidence of positive effects, while exaggerating and generalising the evidence of negative effects. This is scaremongering – and it does not promote healthy social media use. We would not liken giving children sweets to giving children drugs, even though having sweets for every meal could

have serious health consequences. We should therefore not liken social media to drugs either.[4]

Similarly, we must reject the impulse to ask users to "just adapt" to distraction: to bear the burdens of impossible self-regulation, to suddenly become superhuman and take on the armies of industrialized persuasion. To do so would be akin to saying, "Thousands of the world's brightest psychologists, statisticians, and designers are now spending the majority of their waking lives figuring out how to tear down your willpower – so you just need to have more willpower." We must also reject the related temptation to say, "Oh well, perhaps the next generation will be better adjusted to this attentional warfare by virtue of having been born into it." That is acquiescence, not engagement.

Additionally, education is necessary – but not sufficient – for transcending this problem. Nor will "media literacy" alone lead us out of this forest. It's slightly embarrassing to admit this, but back when I was working at Google I actually printed out the Wikipedia article titled "List of Cognitive Biases" and thumb-tacked it on the wall next to my desk. I thought that having it readily accessible might help me be less susceptible to my own cognitive limitations. Needless to say, it didn't help at all.

Nor can we focus on addressing the negative effects the attention economy has on children to the exclusion of addressing the effects it has on adults. This is often the site of the most unrestrained and counterproductive moralizing. To be sure, there are unique developmental considerations at play when it comes to children. However, we should seek not only to protect the most vulnerable members of society, but also the most vulnerable parts of ourselves.

We also can't expect companies to self-regulate, or voluntarily refrain from producing the full effects they're organizationally structured and financially incentivized to produce. Above all, we must not put any stock whatsoever in the notion that advancing "mindfulness" among employees in the technology industry is in any way relevant to or supportive of reforming the dynamics of the digital attention economy. The hope, if not the expectation, that technology design will suddenly come into alignment with human well-being if only enough CEOs and product managers and user experience researchers begin to conceive of it in Eastern religious terms is as dangerous as it is futile. This merely translates the problem into a rhetorical and philosophical frame that is unconnected to the philosophical foundations of Western liberal democracy, and thus is powerless to guide it. The primary function of thinking and speaking in this way is to gesture in the direction of morality while allowing enough conceptual haze and practical ambiguity to permit the impression that one has altered one's moral course while not actually having done so.

Perhaps most of all, we cannot put the blame for these problems on the designers of the technologies themselves. No one becomes a designer or engineer because they want to make people's lives *worse*. Tony Fadell, the founder of the company Nest, has said,

> I wake up in cold sweats every so often thinking, what did we bring to the world? ... Did we really bring a nuclear bomb with information that can – like we see with fake news – blow up people's brains and reprogram them? Or did we bring light to people who never had information, who can now be empowered?[5]

Ultimately, *there is no one to blame*. At "fault" are more often the emergent dynamics of complex multiagent systems rather than the internal decision-making dynamics of a single individual. As W. Edwards Deming said, "A bad system will beat a good person every time."[6] John Steinbeck captured well the frustration we feel when our moral psychology collides with the hard truth of organizational reality in *The Grapes of Wrath*, when tenant farmers are evicted by representatives of the bank:

> "Sure," cried the tenant men, "but it's our land ... We were born on it, and we got killed on it, died on it. Even if it's no good, it's still ours ... That's what makes ownership, not a paper with numbers on it."

"We're sorry. It's not us. It's the monster. The bank isn't like a man."

"Yes, but the bank is only made of men."

"No, you're wrong there – quite wrong there. The bank is something else than men. It happens that every man in a bank hates what the bank does, and yet the bank does it. The bank is something more than men, I tell you. It's the monster. Men made it, but they can't control it."[7]

The bank isn't like a man, nor is the technology company, nor is any other brand nor signifier that we might use to represent the boundary conditions of these technologies that shape our lives. *There is no one to blame*. Knowing this, however, presents us with a choice of two paths. Do we conjure up an image of a "monster" at whom to direct our blame, and take a path which, while psychologically rewarding, is likely to distract from the goal of enacting real change in the real world? Or do we take the second path, and look head-on at the true nature of the system, as messy and psychologically indigestible as it seems to be?

The first path would seem to lead us toward a kind of digital mythology, in which we engage in imagined relationships with personified dynamics of our informational environment, much as the ancients did with their physical and emotional environments.[8] Yet if we take autonomy seriously, we cannot help but note that in Steinbeck's example it is not the displaced farmers, but rather the bankers, who invoke the idea and, we might say, the *brand* of the "monster." Similarly, in the realm of digital technology, it is less often users than companies who produce the representations that serve as the primary psychological and emotional points of connection. In fact, these brands and representations may be the elements of technology design over which users have the least amount of control of all. What this path would entail, then, is acquiescence to a mythology that, while psychologically satisfying, would be (and in many cases already is) even more engineered than the products they represent, or than the decisions that those products are designed to induce.

The second path would entail looking the "monster" in the eye, and seeing it for the complex and multifaceted environment that it is. Such an approach would be akin to what the philosopher Luciano Floridi has called "infraethics," or attention to the infrastructural, "first-order framework of implicit expectations, attitudes, and prac-tices that *can* facilitate and promote morally good decisions and actions."[9] In a sense, the perspective of infraethics views society itself as a sort of persuasive technology, with a persuasive design goal of maximizing moral actions.

None of this implies, however, that we can simply stand by and expect the attention economy to fix itself. Noble mission statements and inspirational marketing claims can neither produce nor substitute for right design. "Some of the major disasters of mankind," writes Alfred North Whitehead, "have been produced by the narrowness of men with a good methodology."[10] Similarly, countertechnologies and calls for players in the attention economy to voluntarily reform may serve as bandages that temporarily stem some localized bleeding – but they are not the surgery, the sustainable systemic change, that is ultimately needed. Besides, they implicitly grant that first, fatal assumption we have already roundly rejected: that it's acceptable for the technologies that shape our thinking and behavior to be in an adversarial relationship against us in the first place.

After acknowledging and avoiding these pitfalls, what route remains? The route in which we take on the task of Herbert Marcuse's "great refusal," which Tim Wu describes in *The Attention Merchants* as being "the protest against unnecessary repression, the struggle for the ultimate form of freedom – 'to live without anxiety.'"[11] The route that remains is the route in which we move urgently to assert and defend our freedom of attention.

NOTES

1 Hegel, Georg W. F. (1820). *Elements of the Philosophy of the Right*. Berlin.
2 Schull, Natasha D. (2012). *Addiction by Design: Machine Gambling in Las Vegas*. Princeton University Press.

3 Pells, Rachael (2017). Giving your Child a Smartphone is Like Giving them a Gram of Cocaine, Says Top Addiction Expert. *Independent*, June 7. www.independent.co.uk/news/education/education-news/child-smart-phones-cocaine-addiction-expert-mandy-saligari-harley-street-charter-clinic-technology-a7777941.html

4 Przybylski, Andy and Orben, Amy (2017). Social Media is Nothing Like Drugs, Despite all the Horror Stories. The Conversation, June 18. https://theconversation.com/social-media-is-nothing-like-drugs-despite-all-the-horror-stories-79382

5 Schwab, Katharine (2017). Nest Founder: "I Wake Up in Cold Sweats Thinking, What Did We Bring To the World?" Co.Design, July 7. www.fastcodesign.com/90132364/nest-founder-i-wake-up-in-cold-sweats-thinking-what-did-we-bring-to-the-world

6 Deming, W. Edward (1993). Deming Four-Day Seminar. Phoenix, Arizona.

7 Steinbeck, John (1939). *The Grapes of Wrath.*

8 Rader, Emilee and Gray, Rebecca (2015). Understanding User Beliefs About Algorithmic Curation in the Facebook News Feed. *Proceedings of the 33rd Annual ACM Conference on Human Factors in Computing Systems – CHI '15* (pp. 173–182). New York, NY: ACM Press.

9 Floridi, Luciano (2017). Infraethics – On the Conditions of Possibility of Morality. *Philosophy and Technology*, 30 (4), 391–394.

10 Whitehead, Alfred N. (1929). *The Function of Reason*. Boston, MA: Beacon Press, 1971.

11 Wu, Tim (2016). *The Attention Merchants: The Epic Scramble to Get Inside Our Heads*. New York, NY: Alfred A. Knopf.

12 Marginal People on Marginal Time

How can we begin to assert and defend our freedom of attention? One thing is clear: it would be a sad reimposition of the same technocratic impulse that gave us the attention economy in the first place if we were to assume that there exists a prescribable basket of "solutions" which, if we could only apply them faithfully, might lead us out of this crisis. There are no maps here, only compasses. There are no three-step templates for revolutions.

We can, however, describe the broad outline of our goal: it's to bring the technologies of our attention onto our side. This means aligning their goals and values with our own. It means creating an environment of incentives for design that leads to the creation of technologies that are aligned with our interests from the outset. It means being clear about what we want our technologies to do for us, as well as expecting that they be clear about what they're designed to do for us. It means expecting our technologies to proceed from a place of understanding about our own views of who we are, what we're doing, and where we're going. It means expecting our technologies and their designers to give attention to, to care about, the right things. If we move in the right direction, then our fundamental understanding of what technology is *for*, as the philosopher Charles Taylor has put it, "will of itself be limited and enframed by an ethic of caring."[1]

Drawing on this broad view of the goal, we can start to identify some vectors of rebellion against our present attentional serfdom. I don't claim to have all, or even a representative set, of the answers here. Nor is it clear to me whether an accumulation of incremental improvements will be sufficient to change the system; it may be that some more fundamental reboot of it is necessary. Also, I won't spend much time here talking about who in society bears responsibility for putting each form of attentional rebellion into place: that will vary widely between issues and contexts, and in many cases those answers aren't even clear yet.

Prior to any task of systemic reform, however, there's one extremely pressing question that deserves as much of our attention as we're able to give it. That question is whether there exists a "point of no return" for human attention (in the deep sense of the term as I have used it here) in the face of this adversarial design. That is to say, is there a point at which our essential capacities for life navigation might be so undermined that we would become unable to regain them and boot-strap ourselves back into a place of general competence? In other words, is there a "minimum viable mind" we should take great pains to preserve? If so, it seems a task of the highest priority to understand what that point would be, so that we can ensure we do not cross it. In conceiving of such a threshold – that is, of the minimally necessary capacities worth protecting – we may find a fitting precedent in what Roman law called the "benefit of competence," or *beneficium compe-tentiae*. In Rome, when a debtor became insolvent and couldn't pay his debts, there was a portion of his belongings that couldn't be taken from him in lieu of payment: property such as his tools, his personal effects, and other items necessary to enable a minimally acceptable standard of living, and potentially even to bootstrap himself back into a position of thriving. This privileged property that couldn't be confiscated was called his "benefit of competence." Absent the "benefit of compe-tence," a Roman debtor might have found himself ruined, financially destitute. In the same way, if there is a "point of no return" for human attention, a "minimum viable mind," then absent a "benefit of com-petence" we could also find ourselves ruined, attentionally destitute. And we are not even debtors: we are serfs in the attentional fields of our digital technologies. They are in *our* debt. And they owe us, at absolute minimum, the benefit of competence.

There are a great number of interventions that could help move the attention economy in the right direction. Any one could fill a whole book. However, four particularly important types I'll briefly discuss here are: (a) rethinking the nature and purpose of advertising, (b) conceptual and linguistic reengineering, (c) changing the upstream determinants of design, and (d) advancing mechanisms for account-ability, transparency, and measurement.

If there's one necessary condition for meaningful reform of the atten-tion economy, it's the reassessment of the nature and purpose of advertising. It's certainly no panacea, as advertising isn't the only incentive driving the competition for user attention. It is, however, by far the largest and most deeply ingrained one.

What is advertising *for* in a world of information abundance? As I wrote earlier, the justification for advertising has always been given on the basis of its informational merits, and it has historically func-tioned within a given medium as the *exception to the rule* of infor-mation delivery: for example, a commercial break on television or a billboard on the side of the road. However, in digital media, advertis-ing now *is* the rule: it has moved from "underwriting" the content and design goals to "overwriting" them. Ultimately, we have no concep-tion of what advertising is *for* anymore because we have no coherent definition of what advertising *is* anymore.[2]

As a society, we ought to use this state of definitional confusion as the opportunity to help advertising resolve its existential crisis, and to ask what we ultimately want advertising to do for us. We must be particularly vigilant here not to let precedent serve as justification. As Thomas Paine wrote in *Common Sense*, "a long habit of not thinking a thing wrong, gives it a superficial appearance of being right."[3] The presence of a series of organizations dedicated to a task can in no sense be justification for that task. (See, e.g., the tobacco industry.) What forms of attitudinal and behavioral manipulation shall we consider to be acceptable business models? On what basis do we regard the wholesale capture and exploitation of human attention as a natural or desirable thing? To what standards ought we hold the mechanisms of commercial persuasion, knowing full well that they will inevitably be used for political persuasion as well?

A reevaluation of advertising's *raison d'etre* must necessarily occur in synchrony with the resuscitation of serious advertising ethics. Advertising ethics has never really guided or restrained the practice of advertising in any meaningful way: it's been a sleepy, tokenistic undertaking. Why has this been so? In short, because advertisers have found ethics threatening, and ethicists have found advertising boring. (I know, because I have been both.)

In advertising parlance, the phrase "remnant inventory" refers to a publisher's unpurchased ad placements, that is, the ad slots of *de minimis* value left over after advertisers have bought all the slots they wanted to buy. In order to fill remnant inventory, publishers sell it at extremely low prices and/or in bulk. One way of viewing the field of advertising ethics is as the "remnant inventory" in the intellectual worlds of advertisers and ethicists alike.

This general disinterest in advertising ethics is doubly surprising in light of the verve that characterized voices critical of the emerging persuasion industry in the early to mid twentieth century. Notably, several of the most prominent early critical voices were veterans of the advertising industry. In 1928, brand advertising luminary Theodore MacManus published an article in the *Atlantic Monthly* titled "The Nadir of Nothingness" that explained his change of heart about the practice of advertising: it had, he felt, "mistaken the surface silliness for the sane solid substance of an averagely decent human nature."[4] A few years later, in 1934, James Rorty, who had previously worked for the McCann and BBDO advertising agencies, penned a missive titled *Our Master's Voice: Advertising*, in which he likewise expressed a sense of dread that advertising was increasingly violating some fundamental human interest:

> [Advertising] is never silent, it drowns out all other voices, and it suffers no rebuke, for is it not the voice of America? ... It has taught us how to live, what to be afraid of, how to be beautiful, how to be loved, how to be envied, how to be successful ... Is it any wonder that the American population tends increasingly to speak, think, feel in terms

of this jabberwocky? That the stimuli of art, science, religion are progressively expelled to the periphery of American life to become marginal values, cultivated by marginal people on marginal time?[5]

The prose of these early advertising critics has a certain tone, well embodied by this passage, that for our twenty-first-century ears is nearly impossible to ignore. It's a sort of pouring out of oneself, an expression of disbelief and even offense at the perceived aesthetic and moral violations of advertising, and it's further tinged by a plaintive, interrogative style that reminds us of other Depression-era writers (James Agee in particular comes to mind). But it reminds me of Diogenes, too: when he said he thought the most beautiful thing in the world was "freedom of speech," the Greek word he used was *parrhesia*, which doesn't just mean "saying whatever you want" – it also means speaking boldly, saying it all, "spilling the beans," pouring out the truth that's inside you. That's the sense I get from these early critics of advertising. In addition, there's a fundamental optimism in the mere fact that serious criticism is being leveled at advertising's existential foundations *at all*. Indeed, reading Rorty today requires a conscious effort not to project our own rear-view cynicism on to him.

While perhaps less poetic, later critics of advertising were able to more cleanly circumscribe the boundaries of their criticism. One domain in which neater distinctions emerged was the logistics of advertising: as the industry matured, it advanced in its language and processes. Another domain that soon afforded more precise language was that of psychology. Consider Vance Packard, for instance, whose critique of advertising, *The Hidden Persuaders* (1957), had the benefit of drawing on two decades of advances in psychology research after Rorty. Packard writes: "The most serious offense many of the depth manipulators commit, it seems to me, is that they try to invade the privacy of our minds. It is this right to privacy in our minds – privacy to be either rational or irrational – that I believe we must strive to protect."[6]

Packard and Rorty are frequently cited in the same neighborhood in discussions of early advertising criticism. In fact, the frequency with which they are jointly invoked in contemporary advertising ethics research invites curiosity. Often, it seems as though this is the case not so much for the content of their criticisms, nor for their antecedence, but for their tone: as though to suggest that, if someone were to express today the same degree of unironic concern about the foundational aims of the advertising enterprise as they did, and to do so with as much conviction, it would be too embarrassing, quaint, and optimistic to take seriously. Perhaps Rorty and Packard are also favored for their perceived hyperbolizing, which makes their criticism easier to dismiss. Finally, it seems to me that anchoring discussions about advertising's fundamental ethical acceptability in the distant past may have a rhetorical value for those who seek to preserve the status quo; in other words, it may serve to imply that any ethical questions about advertising's fundamental acceptability have long been settled.

My intuition is that the right answers here will involve moving advertising away from *attention* and towards *intention*. That is to say, in the desirable scenario advertising would not seek to capture and exploit our mere *attention*, but rather support our *intentions*, that is, advance the pursuit of our reflectively endorsed tasks and goals.

Of course, we will not reassess, much less reform, advertising overnight. Until then, we must staunchly defend, and indeed enhance, people's ability to decline the harvesting of their attention. Right now, the practice currently called "ad blocking" is one of the only ways people have to cast a vote against the attention economy. It's one of the few tools users have if they want to push back against the perverse design logic that has cannibalized the soul of the web. Some will object and say that ad blocking is "stealing," but this is nonsense: it's no more stealing than walking out of the room when the television commercials come on. Others may say it's not prudent to escalate the "arms race" – but it would be fantastic if there were anything remotely resembling an advertising arms race going on. What we have instead is, on one side, an entire industry spending billions of dollars trying to capture your attention using the most sophisticated computers in the world, and on the other side ... your attention. This is more akin to a soldier seeing an army of thousands of tanks and guns advance upon him, and running into a bunker for refuge. It's not an arms race – it's a quest for attentional survival.

The right of users to exercise and protect their freedom of attention by blocking any advertising they wish should be absolutely defended. In fact, given the moral and political crisis of the digital attention economy, the relevant ethical question here is not "Is it okay to block ads?" but rather, "Is it a moral obligation?" This is a question for companies, too. Makers of digital technology hardware and software ought to think long and hard about their obligations to their users. I would challenge them to come up with any good reasons why they shouldn't ship their products with ad blocking enabled by default. Aggressive computational persuasion should be opt-in, not opt-out. The default setting should be one of having control over one's own attention.

Another important bundle of work involves reengineering the language and concepts of persuasive design. This is necessary not only for talking clearly about the problem, but also for advancing philosophical and ethical work in this area. Deepening the language of "attention" and "distraction" to cover more of the human will has been part of my task here. Concepts from neuroethics may also be of help in advancing the ethics of attention, especially in describing the problem and the nature of its harms, as in, for example, the concepts of "brain privacy" or "cognitive liberty."[7]

For companies, a key piece of this task involves reengineering the way we talk about users. Designers and marketers routinely use terms like "eyeballs," "funnels," "targeting," and other words that are perhaps not as humanized as they ought to be. The necessary corrective is to find more human words for human beings. To put a design spin on Wittgenstein's quote from earlier, we might say that the limits of our language mean the limits of our empathy for users.

Regarding the language of "persuasion" itself, there is a great deal of clarification, as well as defragmentation across specific contexts of persuasion, that needs to occur. For example, we could map the language of "persuasive" technologies according to certain ethically salient criteria, as seen in the figure below, where the Y axis indicates the level of constraint the design places on the user and the X axis indicates the degree of alignment between the user's goals and the technology's goals. Using this framework, then, we could describe a technology with a low level of goal alignment and a high degree of constraint as a "Seductive Technology" – for example, an addictive game that a user wants to stop playing, and afterward regrets having spent time on. However, if its degree of constraint were very low, we could instead call it an "Invitational Technology." Similarly, a technology that imposes a low degree of constraint on the user and is highly aligned with their goals, such as a GPS device, would be a "Directive Technology." As its constraints on the user increase, it would become a "Guidance Technology" (e.g. a car's assisted-parking or autopilot features) and at even higher levels a "Driving Technology" (e.g. a fully autonomous vehicle). This particular framework is an initial, rough example for demonstrating what I mean, but it illustrates some of the ways such a project of linguistic and conceptual defragmentation could go.

Degree of constraint	Seduce	Demand	Drive
	Tempt	Persuade	Guide
	Invite	Suggest	Direct

Level of goal alignment between user and Persuasive Technology

Clarifying the language of persuasion will have the added benefit of ensuring that we don't implicitly anchor the design ethics of attention and persuasion in questions of *addiction*. It's understandable why discussion about these issues has already seized on addiction as a core problem: the fundamental challenge we experience in a world of information abundance is a challenge of self-control, and the petty design habits of the attention economy often target our reward system, as I described in Chapter 4.

But there are problems with giving too much focus to the question of addiction. For one, there's a strict clinical threshold for addiction, but then there's also the colloquial use of the term, as shorthand for "I use this technology more than I want to." Without clear definitions, it's easy for people to talk past one another. In addition, if we give too much focus to addiction there's the risk that it could implicitly become a default threshold used to determine whether a design is morally problematic or not. But there are many ways a technology can be ethically problematic; addiction is just one. Even designs that create merely compulsive, rather than "addictive," behaviors can still pose serious ethical problems. We need to be especially vigilant about this sort of ethical scope creep in deployments of the concept of addiction because there are incentives for companies and designers to lean into it: not only does this set the ethical threshold at a high as well as vague level, but it also serves to deflect ethical attention away from deeper ethical questions about goal and value misalignments between the user and the design. In other words, keeping the conversation focused on questions of addiction serves as a convenient distraction from deeper questions about a design's fundamental purpose.

Interventions with the highest leverage would likely involve changing the upstream determinants of design. This could come from, for instance, the development and adoption of alternate corporate structures that give companies the freedom to balance their financial goals with social good goals, and then offer incentives for companies to adopt these corporate structures. (For instance, Kickstarter recently transitioned to become a "benefit corporation," or B-corp. The writer and Columbia professor Tim Wu has recently called in the *New York Times* for Facebook to do the same.)[8] Similarly, investors could create a funding environment that disincentivizes startup companies from pursuing business models that involve the mere capture and exploitation of user attention. In addition, companies could be expected (or compelled, if necessary) to give users a choice about how to "pay" for content online – that is, with their money or with their attention.

Many of these upstream determinants of design may be addressed by changes in the policy environment. Policymakers have a crucial role to play in responding to the crisis of the digital attention economy. To be sure, they have several headwinds working against them: the internet's global nature means local policies can only reach so far, and the rapid pace of technological change tends to result in reactive, rather than proactive, policymaking. But one of the strongest headwinds for policy is the persistence of *informational*, rather than *attentional*, emphases. Most digital media policy still arises out of assumptions that fail to sufficiently account for Herbert Simon's observation about how information abundance produces attention scarcity. Suggestions that platforms be required to tag "fake news," for example, would be futile, an endless game of epistemic whack-a-mole. Initial research has already indicated as much.[9] Similarly, in the European Union, website owners must obtain consent from each user whose browsing behavior they wish to measure via the use of tracking "cookies." This law is intended to protect user privacy and increase transparency of data collection, both of which are laudable aims when it comes to the ethics of *information* management. However, from the perspective of *attention* management, the law burdens users with, say, thirty more decisions per day (assuming they access thirty websites per day) about whether or not to consent to being "cookied" by a site they may have never visited before, and therefore don't know whether or not they can trust. This amounts to a nontrivial strain on their cognitive load that far outweighs any benefit of giving their "consent" to have their browsing behavior measured. I place the word "consent" in quotes here because what inevitably happens is that the "cookie consent" notifications that websites show to users simply become designed to maximize compliance: website owners simply treat the request for "consent" as one more persuasive interaction, and deploy the same methods of measurement and experimentation they use to optimize their advertising-oriented design in order to manufacture users' consent.

However, governmental bodies are uniquely positioned to host conversations about the ways new technological affordances relate to the moral and political underpinnings of society, as well as to advance existential questions about the nature and purpose of societal institutions. And, importantly, they are equipped to foster these conversations in a context that can, in principle, inform and catalyze corrective action. We can find some reasons to be at least cautiously optimistic in precedents for legal protection of attention enacted in predigital media. Consider, for instance, anti-spam legislation and "do not call" registries, which aim to forestall unwanted intrusions into people's private spaces. While protections of this nature generally seek to protect "attention" in the narrow sense – in other words, to mitigate annoyance or momentary distractions – they can nonetheless serve as doorways to protecting the deeper forms of "attention" that I have discussed here.

What can policy do in the near term that would be high-leverage? Develop and enforce regulations and/or standards about the transparency of persuasive design goals in digital media. Set standards for the measurement of certain sorts of attentional harm – that is, quantify their "pollution" of the *inner* environment – and require that digital media companies measure their effects on these metrics and report on them periodically to the public. Perhaps even charge companies something like carbon offsets if they go over a certain amount – we might call them "attention offsets." Also worth exploring are possibilities for digital media platforms that would play a role analogous to the role public broadcasting has played in television and radio.

Advancing accountability, transparency, and measurement in design is also key. For one, having transparency of persuasive design goals is essential for verifying that our trust in the creators of our technologies is well placed. So far, we've largely demanded transparency about the ways technologies manage our *information*, and comparatively less about the ways they manage our *attention*. This has foregrounded issues such as user privacy and consent, issues which, while important, have distracted us from demanding transparency about the design logic – the ultimate *why* – that drives the products and services we use. The practical implication of this is that we've had minimal and shaky bases for trust. "Whatever man you meet," advised the Roman emperor Marcus Aurelius in his *Meditations*, "say to yourself at once: 'what are the principles this man entertains as goods and ills?'"[10] This is good advice not only upon encountering persuasive people, but persuasive technologies as well. What is Facebook's persuasive goal for me? On what basis does YouTube suggest that I watch one video and not another? What metric does Twitter aim to maximize with my time use? Why *did* Amazon build Alexa, after all? Do the goals my trusted systems have for me align with the goals I have for myself? There's nothing wrong with trusting the people behind our technologies, nor do we need perfect knowledge of their motivations to justifiably do so. Trust always involves taking *some* risk. Rather, our aim should be to find a way, as the Russian maxim says, to "trust, but verify."

Equipping designers, engineers, and businesspeople with effective "commitment devices" may also be of use. One common example is that of professional oaths. The oath occupies a unique place in contemporary society: it's weightier than a promise, more universal than a pledge, and more individualized than a creed. Oaths express and remind us of common ethical standards, provide opportunities for making public commitments to particular values, and enable accountability for action. Among the oaths that are not legally binding, the best known is probably the Hippocratic Oath, some version of which is commonly recited by doctors when they graduate from medical school. Karl Popper (in 1970)[11] and Joseph Rotblat (in 1995),[12] among others, have proposed similar oaths for practitioners of science and engineering, and in recent years proposals for oaths specific to digital technology design have emerged as well.[13] So far, none of these oaths have enjoyed broad uptake. The reasons for this likely include the voluntary nature of such oaths, as well as the inherent challenge of agreeing on and articulating common values in pluralistic societies. But the more significant headwinds here may originate in the decontextualized ways in which these proposals have been made. If a commitment device is to be adopted by a group, it must carry meaning for that group. If that meaning doesn't include some sort of *social* meaning, then achieving adoption of the commitment device is likely to be extremely challenging. Most oaths in wide use today depend on some social structure below the level of the profession as a whole to provide this social meaning. For instance, mere value alignment among doctors about the life-saving goals of medicine would not suffice to achieve continued, widespread recitations of the Hippocratic Oath. The essential infrastructure for this habit lies in the social structures and traditions of educational institutions, especially their graduation ceremonies. Without a similar social infrastructure to enable and perpetuate use of a "Designer's Oath," significant uptake seems doubtful.

It could be argued that a "Designer's Oath" is a project in search of a need, that none yet exists because it would bring no new value. Indeed, other professions and practices seem to have gotten along perfectly fine without common oaths to bind or guide them. There is no "Teacher's Oath," for example; no "Fireman's Oath," no "Carpenter's Oath." It could be suggested that "design" is a level of abstraction too broad for such an oath because different domains of design, whether architecture or software engineering or advertising, face different challenges and may prioritize different values. In technology design, the closest analogue to a widely adopted "Designer's Oath" we have seen is probably the voluntary ethical commitments that have been made at the organizational level, such as company mottos, slogans, or mission statements. For example, in Google's informal motto, "do no evil," we can hear echoes of that Hippocratic maxim, *primum non nocere* ("first, do no harm").[14]

But *primum non nocere* does not, in fact, appear in any version of the Hippocratic Oath. The widespread belief otherwise provides us with an important signal about the perceived versus the actual value of oaths in general. A significant portion of their value comes not from their content but from their mere existence: from the societal recognition that a particular practice or profession is oath-*worthy*, that it has a significant impact on people's lives such that *some* explicit ethical standard has been articulated to which conduct within the field can be held.

Assuming we could address these wider challenges that limit the uptake of a "Designer's Oath" within society, what form should such an oath take? In this space, I can only gesture toward a few of the main questions – let alone arrive at any clear answers. One of the key questions is how explicitly such an oath should draw on the example of the Hippocratic Oath. In my view, the precedent seems appropriate to the extent that using the metaphor of medicine to talk about design can help people better understand the seriousness of design. Comparing design to medicine is a useful way of conveying the depth of what is ultimately at stake. Medicine is also an appropriate metaphor because, like design, it's a profession rather than an organization or institution, which makes it an appropriate level of society at which to draw a comparison.

However, one limitation of drawing on medicine as a rough guide to this terrain pertains to the logistics of when and where (and by whom) a "Designer's Oath" would be taken. Medical training is highly systematized, and provides an organizational context for taking such an oath. A technology designer, by contrast, may have never had *any* formal design education – and even those who have, may have never taken a design ethics class. Even for those who *do* take design ethics classes (which are often electives), there is unlikely to be a moment in them when, as in a graduation ceremony, it would not feel extremely awkward to take an oath. Of course, this assumes that an educational setting is the appropriate context for such an oath to begin with. Should we instead look to companies to lead the way? If so, this would raise the further question about *who* should be expected, and not expected, to take the oath (e.g. front-end vs. back-end designers, hands-on designers vs. design researchers, senior vs. junior designers, etc.). Finally, there's also the question of *how* such an oath should be written, especially in the digital age. Should it be a "wiki"-style oath, the product of numerous contributors' input and discussion? Or is such a "crowd-sourced" approach, while an appropriate way to converge on the provisional truth of a *fact* (as in Wikipedia), an undesirable way to develop a clear-minded expression of a moral *ideal*? In any event, we should expect that any "Designer's Oath" receiving wide adoption would continually be iterated and adapted in response to local contexts and new advances in ethical thought, as has been the case with the Hippocratic Oath over many centuries.

As regards the *substance* of a "Designer's Oath" – an initial "alpha" version that can serve as a "minimum viable product" to build upon – I suggest that a good approach would look something like the following (albeit far more poetic and memorable than this):

As someone who shapes the lives of others, I promise to:

> **Care** genuinely about their success;
> **Understand** their intentions, goals, and values as completely as possible;
> **Align** my projects and actions with their intentions, goals, and values;
> **Respect** their dignity, attention, and freedom, and never use their own weaknesses against them;
> **Measure** the full effect of my projects on their lives, and not just those effects that are important to me;
> **Communicate** clearly, honestly, and frequently my intentions and methods; and
> **Promote** their ability to direct their own lives by encouraging reflection on their own values, goals, and intentions.

I won't attempt here to justify each element I've included in this "alpha" version of the oath, but will only note that: (a) it assumes a patient-centered, rather than an agent-centered, perspective; (b) in keeping with the theme of this inquiry, it emphasizes ethical questions related to the management of attention (broadly construed) rather than the management of information; (c) it explicitly disallows design that is consciously adversarial in nature (i.e. having aims contrary to those of the user), which includes a great deal of design currently operative in the attention economy; (d) it goes beyond questions of respect or dignity to include an expectation of *care* on the part of the designer; and (e) it views measurement as a key way of operationalizing that care in the context of digital technology design (as I will further discuss below).

Measurement is also key. In general, our goal in advancing measurement should be to measure what we value, rather than valuing what we already measure. Ethical discussions about digital advertising often assume that limiting user measurement is axiomatically desirable due to considerations such as privacy or data protection. These are indeed important ethical considerations, and if we conceive of the user–technology interaction in informational terms then such conclusions may very well follow. Yet if we take an attention-centric perspective, as I have described above, there are ways in which limiting user measurement may complicate the ethics of a situation, and possibly even actively hinder it.

Greater measurement (of the right things) is in principle a good thing. Measurement is the primary means designers and advertisers have of attending to specific users, and as such it can serve as the ground on which conversations, and if necessary interventions, pertaining to the responsibilities of designers may take place.

One key ethical question we should be asking with respect to user measurement is not merely "Is it ethical to collect more information about a user?" (though of course in some situations that is the relevant question), but rather, "What information about the user are we not measuring, that we have a moral obligation to measure?"

What are the right things to measure? One is potential vulner-abilities on the part of users. This includes not only signals that a user might be part of some vulnerable *group* (e.g. children or the mentally disabled), but also signals that a user might have particularly vulner-able *mechanisms*. (For example, a user may be more susceptible to stimuli that draw them into addictive or akratic behavior.) If we deem it appropriate to regulate advertising to children, it is worth asking why we should not similarly regulate advertising that is targeted to "the child within us," so to speak.

Another major area where measurement ought to be advanced is in the understanding of user intent. The way in which search queries function as signals of user intent, for instance, has played a major role in the success of search engine advertising. Broadly, signals of intent can be measured in forward-looking forms (e.g. explicitly expressed in search queries or inferred from user behavior) as well as backward-looking forms (e.g. measures of regret, such as web page "bounce rates"). However, the horizon of this measurement of intent should not stop at low-level *tasks*: it should include higher and longer-term user *goals* as well. The creators of technologies often justify their design decisions by saying they're "giving users what they want." However, this may not be the same as giving users "what they *want* to want." To do that, they need to measure users' higher goals.

Other things worth measuring include the negative effects tech-nologies might have in users' lives – for example, distraction or decreases in their overall well-being – as well as an overall view of the net benefit that the product is bringing to users' lives (as with Couchsurfing.com's "net orchestrated conviviality" metric).[15] One way to begin doing this is by "measuring the mission" – beginning to operationalize in metrics the company's mission statement or purpose for existing, which is something nearly every company has but which hardly any company actually measures their success toward. Finally, companies can measure the broader effects of their advertising efforts on users – not merely those effects that pertain to the advertiser's persuasive goals.

Ultimately, none of these interventions – greater transparency of persuasive design goals, the development of new commitment devices, or advancements in measurement – is enough to create deep, lasting change in the absence of new mechanisms to make users' voices heard in the design process. If we construe the fundamental problem of the attentional economy in terms of attentional *labor* – that as users we're not getting sufficient value for our attentional labor, and the conditions of that labor are unacceptable – we could conceive of the necessary corrective as a sort of "labor union" for the workers of the attention economy, which is to say, all of us. Or, we might construe our attentional expenditure as the payment of an "attention tax," in which case we currently find ourselves subject to attentional taxation without representation. But however we conceive the nature of the political challenge, its corrective must ultimately consist of user representation in the design process. Token inclusion is insufficient: users need to have a *real* say in the design, and *real* power to effect change. At present, users may have partial representation in design decisions by way of market or user experience research. However, the horizon of concern for such work typically terminates at the question of business value; it rarely raises substantive political or ethical considerations, and never functions as anything remotely like an externally transparent accountability mechanism. Of course, none of this should surprise us at all, because it's exactly what the system so far has been designed to do.

I'm often asked whether I'm optimistic or pessimistic about the potential for reform of the digital attention economy. My answer is that I'm neither. The question assumes the relevant task before us is one of prediction rather than action. But that perspective removes our agency; it's too passive.

Some might argue that aiming for reform of the attention economy in the way I've described here is too ambitious, too idealistic, too utopian. I don't think so – at least, it's no more ambitious, idealistic, or utopian than democracy itself. Finally, some might say "it's too late" to do any or all of this. At that, I can only shake my head and laugh. Digital technology has only just gotten started. Consider that it took us 1.4 million years to put a handle on the stone hand axe. The web, by contrast, is fewer than 10,000 *days* old.

NOTES

1 Taylor, Charles (1992). *The Ethics of Authenticity*. Cambridge, MA: Harvard University Press.

2 Richards, Jef I. and Curran, Catharine M. (2002). Oracles on "Advertising": Searching for a Definition. *Journal of Advertising*, 31 (2), 63–77.

3 Paine, Thomas (1776). *Common Sense*.

4 MacManus, Theodore F. (1928). The Nadir of Nothingness. *Atlantic Monthly*, 19 (May), 594–608.

5 Rorty, James (1934). *Our Master's Voice: Advertising*. New York: John Day. Rorty's title refers to *His Master's Voice*, the famous painting of a terrier listening to his dead master's voice being replayed on a wind-up gramophone. The phrase later became the name of a British record company; today, both the phrase and the image persist in the name and logo of the entertainment retail company HMV.

6 Packard, Vance (1957). *The Hidden Persuaders*. London: Longmans, Green, p. 159.

7 Levy, Neil (2007). *Neuroethics*. Cambridge University Press.

8 Manjoo, Farhad and Roose, Kevin (2017). How to Fix Facebook? We Asked 9 Experts. *New York Times*, September 11. www.nytimes.com/2017/10/31/technology/how-to-fix-facebook-we-asked-9-experts.html

9 Schwartz, Jason (2017). Tagging Fake News on Facebook Doesn't Work, Study Says. Politico, September 11. www.politico.com/story/2017/09/11/facebook-fake-news-fact-checks-242567

10 Marcus Aurelius, *Meditations*, 8.14.

11 Popper, Karl (1970). The Moral Responsibility of the Scientist. *Induction, Physics and Ethics* (pp. 329–336). Dordrecht: Springer.

12 Rotblat, Joseph (1995). Nobel Lecture. Remember your Humanity. The Nobel Foundation. www.nobelprize.org/nobel_prizes/peace/laureates/1995/rotblat-lecture.html

13 Designer's Oath. http://designersoath.com/index.html

14 Hippocrates, *Of the Epidemics*, Book I, section 11.5.

15 Edelman, Joe. www.Couchsurfing.com

13 The Brightest Heaven of Invention

O for a Muse of fire, that would ascend / The brightest heaven of invention

Shakespeare, *Henry V*

Let me tell you about two of my favorite YouTube videos. In the first, a father and his family are in their backyard celebrating his birthday. One person hands him his present, and, seeing that someone has begun video-recording the moment, he senses there's something special about it. He takes his time opening the gift, cracking small jokes along the way. He removes the wrapping paper to find a box containing a pair of sunglasses. But these sunglasses aren't meant for blocking out the sunlight: they're made to let people like him, the colorblind, see the colors of the world. He reads the details on the back of the box longer than is necessary, drawing out the process as though trying to delay, as though preparing himself for an experience he knows will overwhelm him. He takes the black glasses out, holds them up, and silently examines them from all directions. Then someone off-camera exclaims, "Put them on!" He does, then immediately looks away from the camera. He's trying to retain his composure, to take this in his stride. But he can't help jolting between everyday items now, because to him they've all been transfigured. He's seeing for the first time the greenness of the grass, the blueness of the sky, the redness of his wife's poinsettias and her lips, finally, and the full brownness of the kids' hair and the flush peach paleness of their faces as they smile and come to him and hug him, his eyes filling with water as he keeps repeating over and over, "Oh, wow. Oh, man."

The second video opens with a top-down view of Earth, over which the International Space Station is hurtling. A piano plays as we fade into the ISS's observation dome, the Cupola, where a mustached man, the Canadian astronaut Chris Hadfield, floats and stares down at Earth, seemingly lost in reflection. The piano downbeats on a minor chord as he turns to the camera and sings the opening line of David Bowie's song *Space Oddity*: "Ground control to Major Tom." He continues singing as he floats down a corridor of wires and lens flares. Then a guitar appears in his hands as laptops float around him, seeming to balance on their wires like cobras. He sings, "Lock your Soyuz hatch and put your helmet on." (In Bowie's version the line is "Take your protein pills and put your helmet on"; Soyuz is the rocket that today takes astronauts to the ISS.) We see Hadfield singing in his padded, closet-sized quarters, singing as he floats through other shafts and rooms, returning time and again to the Cupola, bright with the light of Earth. He comes to the bridge: "Here am I floating in my tin can / Last glimpse of the world / Planet Earth is blue, and there's nothing left to do." (The original line, in Bowie's version, is "there's nothing I can do.") I don't remember when astronauts started to be able to use the internet in space, but in any case this video made me realize that the World Wide Web isn't just worldwide anymore.

At its best, technology opens our doors of perception, inspires awe and wonder in us, and creates sympathy between us. In the 1960s, some people in San Francisco started walking around wearing a button that read, "Why haven't we seen a photo of the earth from space yet?" They realized that this shift in perception – what's sometimes called the "overview effect" – would occasion a shift in consciousness. They were right: when the first photo of Earth became widely available, it turned the ground of nature into the figure, and enabled the environmental movement to occur. It allowed us all to have the perspective of astronauts, who were up in space coining new terms like "earthlight" and "earthrise" from the surface of the Moon. (Though I can't seem to find the reference, I think it might have been the comedian Norm MacDonald who said, "It must have been weird to be the first people ever to say, 'Where's the earth?' 'Oh, there it is.'")

What's needed now is a similar shift – an overview effect, finding the earthlight – for our inner environment. Who knows, maybe space exploration will play a role this time, too. After all, it did go far in giving us a common goal, a common purpose, a common story during a previous turbulent time. As the mythologian Joseph Campbell said, "The modern hero deed must be that of questing to bring to light again the lost Atlantis of the coordinated soul."[1] This is true at both individual and collective levels.

In order to rise to this challenge, we have to lean into the experiences of awe and wonder. (Interestingly, these emotions, like outrage, also tend to go "viral" in the attention economy.) We have to demand that these forces to which our attention is now subject start standing out of our light. This means rejecting the present regime of attentional serfdom. It means rejecting the idea that we're powerless, that our angry impulses must control us, that our suffering must define us, or that we ought to wallow in guilt for having let things get this bad. It means rejecting novelty for novelty's sake and disruption for disruption's sake. It means rejecting lethargy, fatalism, and narratives of us versus them. It means using our transgressions to advance the good. This is not utopianism. This is imagination. And, as anyone with the slightest bit of imagination knows, "imaginary" is not the opposite of "real."

Future generations will judge us not only for our stewardship of the outer environment, but of the inner environment as well. Our current crisis does not only come in the form of rising global temperatures, but also in our injured capacities of attention. Our mission, then, is not only to reengineer the world of matter, but also to reengineer our world so that we can give attention to what matters.

Today, the right sort of redesign is not yet in fashion. My purpose here has been to identify and advance it as best I could in the time and space I had. I have also sought to encourage and guide the attention of others who share my deep concern about this vast infrastructure of technological persuasion we have inherited – but who, also like me, take solace in encountering others on this road who see the same problems, and respond to them with the same vigor of inquiry that I have been fortunate enough to enjoy in the writing of this book.

In order to do anything that matters, we must first be able to give attention to the things that matter. It's my firm conviction, now more than ever, that the degree to which we are able and willing to struggle for ownership of our attention is the degree to which we are free.

NOTES

1 Campbell, Joseph (2008). *The Hero with a Thousand Faces* (vol. XVII). New World Library.

Acknowledgments

Deepest thanks are owed to my wife, brothers, and parents for many years of love and encouragement. I wish to specifically acknowledge the influence of my father, Dr. Rodney Don Williams, a man to whose goodness and wisdom I daily aspire.

I am grateful to many friends, mentors, and colleagues who have helped me develop the ideas contained herein. For essential guidance during the course of my doctoral research, I thank Professor Luciano Floridi and the Digital Ethics Lab at the University of Oxford. I also thank Professor Julian Savulescu and the Oxford Uehiro Centre for Practical Ethics for ongoing feedback on my work. I am also deeply indebted to my friends at Balliol College for countless evenings of lively and well-lubricated debate, in particular Joshua Melville, Achas Burin, and Thomas Møller-Nielsen. I have also greatly benefited from my ongoing alliance with the global Time Well Spent community, in particular conversations with Tristan Harris, Joe Edelman, Max Stossel, and Anika Saigal.

I have also benefited from important conversations with many other formidable minds, among them Victoria Nash, William Dutton, Mariarosaria Taddeo, Tim Wu, Burkhard Schafer, Ralph Schroeder, Vili Lehdonvirta, Eric Meyer, Heather Ford, the DPhil seminars at the Oxford Internet Institute, Roger Crisp, Janet Radcliffe-Richards, Regina Rini, Jeff McMahan and the Oxford Moral Philosophy Seminars, the Oxford Applied Ethics Work in Progress Seminar, Anders Sandberg, Carissa Véliz, Fay Niker, Wael Ghonim, Benson Dastrup, Constantin Vică, and Emilian Mihailov.

This book would never have existed without the encouragement of Ernesto Oyarbide, who informed me about the Nine Dots Prize and nudged me to apply. I am grateful to all those who conceived and carried out the inaugural instance of this unique competition, including: Peter Kadas and the Kadas Prize Foundation; Jane Tinkler; Simon Goldhill and the Centre for Research in the Arts, Social, Sciences, and Humanities at the University of Cambridge; the Nine Dots Prize board members; and Caitlin Allen and Laura Curtis at Riot Communications.

Finally, I thank Chris Harrison and Sarah Payne at Cambridge University Press for their astute editorial guidance, as well as Crystal Lin for her support with elements of the research. I am also grateful to the Oxford *Practical Ethics* Blog, as well as *Quillette* Magazine, in whose pages I developed earlier versions of some ideas that appear in this book.

Further Reading

Crawford, Matthew (2015). *The World Beyond Your Head: How to Flourish in an Age of Distraction*. Harmondsworth: Penguin.

Eyal, Nir (2014). *Hooked: How to Build Habit-Forming Products*. London: Portfolio Penguin.

Huxley, Aldous (1932). *Brave New World*. London: Chatto & Windus.

Huxley, Aldous (1985). *Brave New World Revisited*. New York, NY: Harper & Brothers.

James, William (1983). *The Principles of Psychology. Philosophy and Phenomenological Research* (vol. XLIV). New York: Henry Holt.

Levy, Neil (2007). *Neuroethics: Challenges for the Twenty-first Century*. Cambridge University Press.

Müller, Jan-Werner (2016). *What is Populism?* Philadelphia, PA: University of Pennsylvania Press.

Nussbaum, Martha (2016). *Anger and Forgiveness: Resentment, Generosity, and Justice*. Oxford University Press

Orwell, George (1949). *1984*. London: Secker & Warburg.

Postman, Neil (1987). *Amusing Ourselves to Death*. Harmondsworth: Penguin.

Rousseau, Jean-Jacques (1755; 2009). *A Discourse on Political Economy*. Oxford University Press.

Rousseau, Jean-Jacques (1762; 2009). *The Social Contract*. Oxford University Press.

Index

Printed in the United States
By Bookmasters